NEVER GIVE UP

NEVER GIVE UP

MY LIFE AND GOD'S MERCY

JOHN JANARO

PUBLISHED BY ST. ANTHONY MESSENGER PRESS
CINCINNATI, OHIO

Unless otherwise noted, Scripture passages have been taken from the *Revised Standard Version*, Catholic edition. Copyright 1946, 1952, 1971 by the Division of Christian Education of the National Council of Churches of Christ in the USA. Used by permission. All rights reserved.

Scripture passages marked *NAB* have been taken from *New American Bible*, New York: Catholic Book, 1991.

Note: The editors of this volume have made minor changes in capitalization to some of the Scripture quotations herein. Please consult the original source for proper capitalization.

Cover design by John M. Lucas, LUCAS Art & Design, Jenison, MI
Cover image copyright © Veer Incorporated
Book design by Mark Sullivan

LIBRARY OF CONGRESS CATALOGING-IN-PUBLICATION DATA
Janaro, John.
Never give up : my life and God's mercy / John Janaro.
p. cm.
Includes bibliographical references (p.   ) and index.
ISBN 978-0-86716-929-4 (pbk. : alk. paper) 1. Janaro, John. 2. Suffering—Religious aspects—Catholic Church. 3. Lyme disease—Religious aspects—Catholic Church. 4. Depression, Mental—Religious aspects—Catholic Church. 5. Lyme disease—Patients—Religious life. 6. Depressed persons—Religious life. I. Title.
BX2373.S5J36 2010
248.8'619—dc22
2009040085

ISBN 978-0-86716- 929-4

Published by Servant Books, an imprint of St. Anthony Messenger Press.
28 W. Liberty St.
Cincinnati, OH 45202
www.ServantBooks.org

Printed in the United States of America.

Printed on acid-free paper.

10 11 12 13 14 5 4 3 2 1

For my wife,
who bears me better
than I bear myself.

INTRODUCTION

This little book is a personal testimony, an offering of adoration and gratitude to God, who has sustained me with fidelity and tenderness throughout my confused, distracted, and often difficult life. His divine mercy has become the focus of my life in the midst of many difficulties and sorrows as well as blessings. God indeed has greatly consoled me, and more than once I have glimpsed the mysterious hand of his providence in my life.

I am a husband, a father, a teacher, and a writer. I live in a town that—as far as the human dimension is concerned—is much like any other town. I give to the collection every week but also have received much assistance from the local church, spiritually and materially. I have traveled and have had wonderful experiences, have found satisfaction in my work, and have received immeasurable love from my wife and children.

Over the past nine years I have struggled to come to terms with a chronic and sometimes debilitating case of Lyme disease. I have had to face the physical limitations of pain and disability as well as long periods of loneliness and helplessness, unable to work or pursue any of my other normal activities. The nature of my illness, however, is such that there have also been periods when I have been healthy enough to teach and write, hike in the mountains, fish, swim, and ride a bicycle.

There have been other trials. In 2006 and 2007 one of our children was in the hospital for seven months. Josefina had two major surgeries, and we feared for her life.

Underlying these trials has been a hidden affliction—chronic depression with episodes of obsessive-compulsive disorder—which has caused great difficulty throughout my life.

These sufferings do not indicate that I possess any unusual spiritual depth or wisdom. Indeed, one thing I have learned is that suffering does not automatically make one a better person. It can make a person bitter, cynical, mean spirited, discouraged, envious, and self-centered. It can cause distress in a person's relationship with God, who may seem distant, unresponsive to prayer, and even cold.

Additionally I am convinced that the sufferings of my family in these recent years are nothing more than the lot of multitudes of people throughout our world. They, too, love and struggle and seek the face of God.

We must never lose our trust in God. Even when life is a black abyss, we must have faith, because God has promised, "I am with you" (Isaiah 43:5; Matthew 28:20; see Psalm 23:4). The road is often narrow and dark, but God is our shepherd. He is by our side, even when we feel very much like wounded sheep.

When we walk "through the valley of the shadow of death" (Psalm 23:4), we must not give in to fear—which is to say that we must not give in to the bug of anxiety that would bite us at every turn. "The valley of the shadow" is a long way from paradise. And yet God is with us. We must hold close to him in faith, a faith that comes to life through the breath of love, however faint that breath may seem.

"You are with me; your rod and your staff, they comfort me" (Psalm 23:4). The rod and the staff may prod the sheep; sometimes that is the only thing the sheep can feel in the darkness. The shepherd is determined not to lose the sheep, determined to keep them as close to him as possible, and he uses his rod and staff to keep the sheep from wandering blindly into the thickets of that valley of shadows.

It is probably in the most terrifying and lost moments of the journey, when we are bleeding from running away and rolling in the brambles, that the shepherd raises us up and carries us on his shoulders. We may bleat and thrash and struggle because he locks our legs together in his strong hands. It is good that he is so strong.

We must never lose our trust in God. We must hold on to him, in the midst of the fury, with our understanding that his promise is true. For we know that his mercy is at the end of all things.

This book is a journal of the joys and struggles of my soul in times of trial and a witness in praise and thanksgiving to the God who has never failed me. It is a testament to the attitude of heart that the Lord has formed in me over the course of these years. These words are intensely personal. But the core of the experience from which they spring is common to many, and some may hear in them echoes of their own voices. We are moving forward on a narrow path, where the heart searches for God, for the face of love, and for the power to give itself in love. We need not walk this path alone.

I hope that this book will provide worthwhile reflections for all people who suffer (which is to say, everyone) and in particular for those who suffer from chronic physical disability or mental or emotional illness. My words are also for families, friends, pastors, and spiritual advisors, who can best find their place in suffering people's lives by sharing the path with them.

PART ONE

In the Valley of the Shadow:
A History of My Illness

CHAPTER ONE

Bang!

Lyme disease flares up unexpectedly, often in response to stress: the pressures of too much activity and not enough rest. And so one day I was living my life, feeling pretty well, doing my job, still taking medication (of course) but not realizing how much I depended on it, and then, bang!

There were warning signs: I had been feeling tired. I wasn't sleeping well. I was pushing myself with the preparation and delivery of a special lecture series over a period of several weeks, in addition to various other activities. But as I looked at the paramedics who were taking me from my bed to a stretcher to the ambulance, with red lights flashing in the dark, I was bewildered. "This is not supposed to be happening now. I am fine—except for this pain."

It was not a heart attack but an episode of arrhythmia. Nevertheless my body quickly "caught on," and I became sick in all sorts of other ways. That's life with Lyme disease.

Back home, "I'll shake this off," I thought. "I'll be fine." But my mind felt like a slow-moving cement mixer. Everything around me was normal, but my insides were shutting down.

I returned to my classroom and my students. But when I tried to lecture, bricks came out of my mouth and slammed on the floor. The "bang" seemed like some kind of odd intrusion. Couldn't I just pick up my life where it was before?

No. Not this time. After some seven years of struggling to sustain my teaching career, I had to face the fact that it was over. I was taken out of my life, suddenly, and placed in a dark valley. Not entirely dark—my wife and family were there, and I was in my own house. But I wondered, "What happens now? Where am I? Who am I?" Everyone agreed that I couldn't go on this way.

I am on a new and strange road. It's not quite like death, because there is a future ahead. But where am I going?

CHAPTER TWO

My Visible Illness

In 2007 I was looking back on a twenty-one-year career devoted to the pursuit of truth and to serving the needs of students at a small but growing Catholic college. I had studied theology for six years (including a year in Rome), authored two books, edited books for my college's publishing house and also our quarterly academic journal for six years, and served for two years in the student affairs office as dean of men. I gave my first lectures in 1992 and became an assistant professor of theology in 1994, then was promoted to associate professor in 2000. I served a three-year term as chair of our theology department.

I married my dear wife, Eileen, in 1996. We have five children.

In the midst of this active and even strenuous life, I began in the year 2000 to struggle with the strange, painful, and debilitating symptoms of what turned out to be a long-standing and previously untreated case of Lyme disease. The college, my family, and I tried to find ways to keep me going. Starting in 2005 I took two extended periods of sick leave and carried reduced responsibilities when I was working. Meanwhile I waged war on the illness by enlisting various doctors and trying a whole spectrum of conventional and alternative treatments and therapies. Unfortunately, any relief I gained proved to be temporary and unreliable.

Disability was precisely the word for my situation. I loved my work, probably too much, but it was physically and emotionally draining, and I was struggling with more than just Lyme disease. After seven years of withering stress, temporary remissions, and setbacks, my health was broken.

It was clear that a basic change in my way of life was being imposed on me. It was clear to me in prayer that this was God's will; indeed, I had the sense—sometimes the powerful sense—that he wanted to lead me in a new direction. It was also clear to my wife, my doctors, and the college administration.

Nevertheless, at the time (and even sometimes to this day) I was oppressed by feelings of worthlessness and failure. These feelings, no matter how powerful their grip, do not correspond to what I know to be true. But human beings are complicated creatures, and the story of my afflictions is more complicated than many.

Chronic borreliosis is a technical term for the advanced stage of the infection commonly known as Lyme disease. Acute Lyme, if promptly and properly treated with antibiotics, can be cured fairly easily. If neglected, however, it can develop into this serious, lifelong, painful, and even crippling illness.

Nowadays most of us know a little bit, at least, about Lyme disease. We know that it is transmitted by the bite of a rascally little insect called a tick. We know that it has nothing to do with any kind of substance called lyme, much less that bittersweet green fruit—the lime—that gives flavor to cocktails, salad dressings, and sodas. In fact, the disease is named for the venerable town of Old Lyme, Connecticut, where the first major outbreak of the disease occurred in 1975.

People wonder, is this a new disease? Theories abound on this question and on many others connected with Lyme disease. I am not going to go into any of them here. Medical science is in conflict about the disease, its consequences, how to treat it, how to prevent it, and so on. By the time you read this, opinions may have changed. I'll just note some basic points.

Lyme disease is a spirochete bacterial infection communicated by ticks. (Anyone who spends time outside knows—or should know—what a tick looks like and how to remove one if it latches on to you.) Ticks are carriers of all sorts of unhealthy microorganisms, but one group in particular have revealed themselves to be especially painful scourges among humans in the last forty years: the bacteria classified as *borrelia burgdorferi*.

Borrelia infection can be detected early by a rash around the tick bite or by the onset of joint pain or flulike symptoms. Sometimes the infection is confirmed by blood tests, but due to the unreliability of many of the standard tests and the danger of forgoing immediate treatment, some doctors administer the necessary antibiotics on the strength of a clinical diagnosis. Personally, I think this is a good idea. If the disease is not treated at its acute stage, the initial symptoms will eventually go away, but the bacteria will enter a new phase of infection.

Adaptable and tough to kill at this later stage, the bacteria bore their way into tissues, organs, and even the central nervous system. Serious and chronic illness may begin rapidly. Or the bacteria may dwell dormant in the body for a long time without manifesting any symptoms (such was the case with me), only to reemerge years later, usually in response to a triggering event such as another serious illness, bodily trauma, pregnancy, some other change in the immune system, or any number of as yet unidentified factors.

The revived bacteria are more virulent than they were initially. They can cause a whole spectrum of symptoms that are often mistaken for other rheumatic or neurological illnesses. Joint and muscle pain, exhaustion, cognitive difficulties, neurological and sensory dysfunctions, intensified arthritic degeneration, and the further irritation of other chronic conditions may occur. The infection can spread to vital organs, disrupt their functioning, and even result in fatal complications.

As of this writing, I am not aware of any formal compilation of statistics regarding the contribution of chronic Lyme disease to deaths resulting from brain, heart, lung, kidney, or other vital organ failure. But there is abundant evidence to conclude that it can and does occur.

In 2008 the governor of Virginia declared May "Lyme Disease Awareness Month." Perhaps I was born twenty years too soon. In the spring of 1988, few people in the state of Virginia were aware of Lyme disease. Any doctors who had heard of it thought it a weird phenomenon peculiar to New England and upstate New York.

In 1988 I was a young graduate student who loved to explore the woods and hills of beautiful northern Virginia. I ran into quite a few ticks in those days, as I remember. I would just pull them off and keep going. Nature lovers are always get-

tinue fighting and hoping that treatment options improve, knowing always that my life is in the hands of God.

This is the story of my visible illness. It is the most tangibly difficult and outwardly life-restraining circumstance that I face. But I cannot give an account of who I am, nor an adequate testimony to the wonderful mercy by which God has sustained me, without giving an account of my other illness, the *invisible* one.

CHAPTER THREE

My Invisible Illness

I pondered and prayed a great deal about whether I should include my struggles with depression in this book. After all, Lyme disease provides plenty of material for a book about suffering. But I realized that this book is not primarily about suffering; it is primarily about the mercy of God. Who am I that I should hide the glory of God's mercy?

And there is another reason for including this account of my depression. I feel a responsibility to be a witness for the millions who suffer—too often silently and desperately—from this crippling, suffocating disease.

Long before the pain and drama of Lyme disease came into my life, I carried within myself this *invisible* affliction. Depression is not sadness, or laziness, or a personality flaw. It is a sickness, every bit as much as Lyme disease or cancer.

A lot has been said and written about depression in recent years. There has been, in fact, much progress in the understanding and treatment of it and related psychiatric disorders.

(As I will explain, my own condition is a complex one, with depression as a dominant but not exclusive feature.) Still, a person who has never experienced depression as a real mental, emotional, and physical hindrance to ordinary life may find it difficult to understand it as a *disease*.

Many people assume that depression is the result of the failure of oversensitive people to deal with their problems or weather traumatic circumstances in life. They think that depression results from a lack of personal character or an excess of personal misfortune or some other combination of external and internal circumstances. Indeed, these things can *trigger* depression, but they do not *explain* its structure or its persistent nature.

People who are depressed must be distinguished from people who are simply *discouraged*. If someone's problem is within the normal range of human emotion or human frailty—whether it be discouragement or sloth or fear of responsibility or the overwhelming nature of the circumstances they face—they do not suffer from the disease of depression. (On the other hand, any situation like this should be watched attentively for signs of clinical depression. The interior suffering of the human person is not easily understood and should never be dismissed by a summary judgment.)

When I say that I have depression, I am not referring to a transient emotional state or even to a feeling that has any essential connection to external circumstances. The disease of depression is a long-standing and ongoing affliction that cannot be resolved by circumstances or willpower. Depressed people cannot simply "pull themselves together" and "get over" their condition.

Depression is widely recognized today as a medical condition with a neurological basis. It is a disorder that affects the intricate functioning of neurotransmitters in the brain and the chemicals that balance brain activity. It manifests itself in a broad spectrum of symptoms and with widely varying levels of intensity.

Personally, I believe the time has come to rename psychiatric conditions such as depression in keeping with current scientific knowledge and in order to distinguish them from inadequate and potentially deceptive terminology based only on behavior patterns. I propose that we refer to depression and other such clearly recognized and verifiable conditions as *Neurochemical Imbalance Disorders* (or NIDs). This will help distinguish the tiger from the kitten.

I have suffered from an NID—a complex depression, anxiety, and obsessive-compulsive disorder—since I was a child. I am not "nuts," but I am afflicted with *invisible* sufferings that can interfere with day-to-day life. Scrupulosity, obsessive fears, overwhelming and paralyzing lack of confidence, and a morbid sense of worthlessness—all these have haunted me for as long as I can remember. Fear and a sense of self-loathing alternate with a brain freeze that makes me want to withdraw from all the things in life that I really like.

Depression can bring life to a standstill for no apparent or adequate reason. A mental exhaustion that cannot raise itself even to activities that are fun and easy has no normal explanation in the moral or behavioral realm.

My disorder, thank God, is not always present at an unbearable level of intensity. It has had its flare-ups and its remissions throughout my life. In fact, it acts remarkably like the chronic, physiologically based illness that it really is. It can be triggered by events, stress, other illnesses, overall neglect of my personal health, overwork, poor diet, lack of sleep, and a whole range of other factors—not to mention infections like Lyme disease, which can cross the blood-brain barrier and stir up, exacerbate, or even initiate all sorts of neurological imbalances and disorders.

I do not deny the spiritual foundation of our thoughts and affections. But I insist on something that human beings too often forget: namely, that the human person is a *union* of body and soul. This means that thoughts, impressions, apparent judgments, and emotions can be profoundly *influenced* by the physical condition of that delicate and marvelous instrument, the human brain.

This is not materialism. In fact, the basic insights of today's psychiatric medicine (though not all its conclusions) are remarkably consistent with the Christian understanding of the human person. My point is not that spiritual freedom is *reduced* to the function of the brain. Rather it is that the environment in which spiritual freedom comes into play must take into account the physical context of its circumstances, which include the condition and functioning of the brain.

This is obvious to anyone who has ever been asleep. When you sleep, the functioning of your brain changes, and as a result you are unconscious, or your imagination generates dreams. You may talk or even walk, but your freedom is not involved because of the physical context of sleep.

It is also clear that external substances, such as alcohol, affect the brain and thereby affect thoughts, impressions, and emotions. It should not be hard, therefore, for us to understand how the very complex, internal functioning of the brain can affect our interior environment and shape features of our conscious life. If the brain is affected by a chemical imbalance caused by a disease, it is not surprising that the person suffers from psychological hindrances or even breakdowns.

A person suffering from depression is no more able to "cheer up" or "snap out of it" or think and act "normally" than a person with a broken leg is able to walk normally. No amount of exhortation, encouragement, or willpower can get a person with a broken leg to walk as if he or she doesn't have a broken leg. That person needs medical treatment, therapy, support and help from others in the healing process, and time. The same kind of approach is necessary for a person with depression or any kind of NID.

From all I know about depression and how bad it can be, I would consider my own condition to be no more than moderate. I have never been hospitalized for psychiatric reasons, although there have been episodes in my life for which this might have been helpful. I suffered for years without understanding what was wrong with me. It was only in 1994 that I discovered that depression could be treated with medication, with intelligent therapy grounded in a solid practical grasp of human nature, with a team of supportive people, and—yes—with prayer and spiritual guidance.

Any illness presents special challenges to the human spirit, and psychiatric disorders, which affect our awareness so intimately, require particular attention. A spiritual director should not reduce the spiritual life to a psychological process but should be *attentive to the fact* that many people today live out their relationship with God within the difficult inner environment engendered by psychiatric illness.

It has been essential for me to discover that this disease is *not who I am*. It does not even correspond to my temperament. It is true that I am an intense person intellectually and emotionally, but my intensity is naturally positive. *I love life*. Depression locks my personality up in a prison. I still have to struggle to live with this disease, and I cannot do it without continued treatment and the support of others.

My experience has opened me up to the reality that there are many people who are in much greater pain than I. I share—in what is really a small way—in the physical, emotional, and mental pains that make the lives of many people an uninterrupted misery. I cannot pretend to fathom this misery, but I know that it exists. And with this empathy I present my own testimony.

Perhaps I can speak for many who suffer in silence, who are not understood by their loved ones or who do not even understand themselves. They feel imprisoned by pain of brain and body. Their plight is not a plague in a faraway country, nor does it appear in the news. These people are in our neighborhoods, schools, and offices, and too often no one hears their pleas for care and compassion. Perhaps my testimony can help them—and help others understand them. I shall entrust that possibility, with faith and prayer, to the grace and wisdom of God.

CHAPTER FOUR

The Cloud

Depression has many facets. In what follows I am going to try to get to the root of how it has afflicted me and describe it in broad terms.

I have lived my whole life inside a strange "cloud" that seeps into my brain as a kind of subconscious premise: *It is bad to be John Janaro*. What is this "cloud," and where does it come from?

The cloud does not come from the devil. The devil certainly makes use of it to tempt me (as do the world and the flesh). "*It is bad to be John Janaro*," says the cloud.

"So why bother praying?" says Screwtape. "God doesn't love you." Or he says, "Forget about God, and *make yourself* good."

The world and the flesh chime in, "Indulge yourself. Do things that make you *feel* good, and don't worry about their consequences for yourself, other people, or God."

And the devil reminds me, "God doesn't care about you anyway. Neither does anyone else."

Then, if I do indulge, disappointment and guilt and self-hatred follow like a wave. And I say to myself, "It *is* bad to be me."

And the devil follows up, "You're right, and you can't do without this badness, you stinker!"

People with depression still have free will. Their condition poses a special challenge that can become a context for sin (but also for growth in love). Having a cloud in the brain that throbs with *"It's bad to be me"* is not a sin. The cloud is a distortion in self-consciousness based in a physical disorder and aggravated by external circumstances.

The central temptation of the devil is his attempt to convince us, "It *is* bad to be you! And it's *your fault!*" This is a big lie. But like all big lies, it has some basis in truth: We are all wounded by original sin, and we are all personal sinners.

The cloud can distort the perception of our own sinfulness. It can also obscure or even obliterate our capacity for free choice, thus diminishing guilt or excusing us altogether. Still, we are human beings, and so we are capable of doing evil like anyone else. And like anyone else, we must repent, confess, and make amends for our sins.

This dark cloud that stunts our self-consciousness, so that we are more or less always thinking or feeling or at least weighted with the subconscious fear that "my existence is worthless," *is imposed by factors outside of our free, acting, personal self.* It is a distortion of perception, which hinders us from seeing ourselves in a true way.

It is true that you can do many bad things and even become *morally* bad. But it is *never* true that you are bad simply because you are you! Your existence is always good; you, as a person, are good. You are loved by God. You have a purpose. You are not worthless, even if you are steeped in sin.

Please understand, I am not trying to make some subtle philosophical point here. This distinction is the line between life and death for a person suffering from depression. I am trying to articulate it as best I can.

I have lived inside this cloud since childhood: *It is a bad thing to be John Janaro*. The cloud could become much darker if other people seemed to confirm this distortion, but in this respect God has blessed me. I grew up in a loving family and had a happy childhood, even with the cloud. I have had many positive and rewarding experiences in my adult life. The main aggravating external factors in my depression are the external physical illnesses that have imposed so many limitations on me.

But the neurological disorder that produces this distorted, negative self-image is the core of the disease. I cannot emphasize enough the fact that the foundation of depression is *physical*.

Not surprisingly, depression runs in my family. My grandfather had it all his life. One of my great aunts spent most of her life in a psychiatric hospital. (This was a long time ago; no doubt she would have received better treatment today.) Other relatives have been afflicted with it. Something is going on here that is more than coincidental.

But many people in my immediate and extended family have never suffered from any problem of this sort. If there is a genetic pattern or predisposition, I don't know how to trace its path. Many people with NIDs have similar family backgrounds.

I praise God for his mercy in my struggle with depression. I have the support of my family and the understanding and patience of my wife. I am being treated and cared for. But the cloud is still there, even though some light has broken through.

How many times I have tried to burst out and just be John Janaro, but I can never do it with fullness and confidence. It involves more than proving to myself and to the world that I have value by virtue of my achievements. After all, I do have a pretty impressive resume. And now that I am sick—which is not my fault—people think that I handle my trials with courage. Maybe sometimes I do. But all of this is a fragile light; the thickness of the cloud remains.

What makes this so hard to explain is that it is not a problem of knowledge or judgment. I *know* that "it is a *good* thing to be John Janaro." The cloud is not fundamentally an error of knowledge or judgment, although it can distort knowledge and lead to erroneous judgments about myself. (Here is a place where good psychotherapy and good spiritual guidance have been very helpful to me.)

The cloud is not even a matter of how I feel. I cannot find the way out by trying to "feel good about myself." This does not get to the root of the problem, and it can lead to a life of constant temporary and superficial distractions.

The cloud is a kind of atmosphere of my everyday awareness. It is a stunted sensibility that pervades my system and that I fall back on whenever any stimulating or distracting or constructive and engaging activity is over.

So will the cloud ever go away? I believe that through the years I have been *partially* healed. Indeed, I give thanks to God for the real measure of healing I am experiencing. This healing is the result of treatment and care (as I have already noted) but also—insofar as I can infer from my own experience—the intervention of God, whose healing mercy flows through many channels in the life of the Church. Prayer and the sacraments bring the love of God to bear on the whole person, in accordance with his mysterious plan.

Founded on baptism and sustained by grace, relationships can be rivers of healing. I pray that people today will discover the power of the sacrament of marriage. God can empower spouses to be instruments of healing to one another. I would truly be lost without my wife and family.

Meanwhile, how do I live with what remains?

This disease is *not who I am*. The recognition of this is essential, but the translation of this judgment into a disposition of the heart requires a continual effort. It requires prayer. I am not entirely healed, which means I must live my relationship with God in the recognition that he wills the cloud to remain in some measure, as part of his loving plan for my life.

By God's grace I have found that depression can be transformed into an awareness of my total dependence on God. I must beg him to continually deepen my awareness of my need for him. The good news, of course, is that he is here to meet that need, that dependence that really *is* who I am. Jesus Christ has united my whole life to his. He is here, in every circumstance, in every difficulty. The cloud says, "I am nothing." Humility says, "I am nothing *without You*."

I noted above that depression can become a context for growing in love. But I don't grow in love simply by figuring this out. It is possible to affirm, as a kind of external idea, that "God loves me" while at the same time being plunged into the cloud. I could write a brilliant theological treatise on the love of God for every human person and still be afflicted and crushed with the sense of being worthless. To grow in love is to grow in the heart.

I can grow because, in fact, Jesus really is here. He takes the initiative. He knows the depths of my sorrow, and he enters into me right there, where I think I am most alone. If I am talking to him (prayer), it is because he is already here. And he knows the language of the heart. He hears and understands my secret cry before I even know that I have made it. He answers, and he promises that he is not going to give up on me. I must never give up on him.

I sense that the cloud is not so big, because—after all—I am rather small.

"You, O God, are good." And the nothingness of me is filled with the goodness of God. That is how it should be.

And so it *is* good to be John Janaro, God's creature, cherished and loved and wanted by him. That is the truth, even though—honestly—it is a daily struggle to say this to myself. But I want to love and glorify the good God who created me and redeemed me. God is present, here and now and always, in Jesus.

"Jesus, make me good. Make me holy. Make me yours."

CHAPTER FIVE

Stuck Inside My Head

As I indicated, there is also an anxiety/obsession side to my NID. At different times it has been diagnosed as obsessive-compulsive disorder (OCD) or the alternate "pole" to my depression (as in a "bipolar" disorder).

OCD belongs to the same family of brain disorders as Tourette's syndrome, the illness characterized by constant involuntary spasms of the head and neck. Obsessiveness must be distinguished from the behavior that arises from an overly meticulous temperament or from the peculiarities that may accompany the pangs of a genuinely guilty conscience. For example, the blood spots Lady Macbeth tries to wash are not real, but the *murder* she has committed is real; for the OCD sufferer *there is no murder*, although he may be hounded by notions that he has committed one or is going to unless he keeps washing his hands.

Thus, as with depression, obsessive thoughts and anxieties are unreal or distorted impressions or emotions that chemical imbalances impose on a person's awareness and inner environment. They are inner spasms that disrupt and even disable a person's conscious life.

I have had obsessions of various kinds since I was a child. I was often overcome by fears of contracting certain diseases by touching certain objects. (I find it a bit ironic that I did eventually become seriously ill from coming into contact with certain objects, that is, ticks.) Obsessions would flare up and torture me for months and then fade for months or even years.

As I got older, certain aspects of the problem became more chronic. Obsessive fears have hindered numerous basic activities. I still have trouble carrying out certain methodical tasks—from filling out forms to using various features of computers and the Internet to following directions in putting something together—all because of the oppressive fear of leaving something out or making mistakes. As a teacher, grading papers was pure torture: "Is this answer right or wrong? What comment should I put on the page? Have I explained that clearly enough?" The strange thing is that my basic common sense is always there in the background, telling me what to do, yet I keep getting *stuck*.

As I learned more about sins, my obsessions began to press on me the notion that somehow I had committed them. Other religious issues can arise—all of a sudden—to torment me. For example, some years ago I began to fear that my marriage was invalid. I obsessed over the possibility that I may have taken religious vows at some point in the past and then *forgotten* about them. I found myself checking canon law books to find out what this would mean. When I discovered that vows could be dispensed, I then conceived the fear that I might have married someone else in the past and then forgotten about it.

All along I *knew* in my mind that none of this had any basis in reality. I knew I had never been married before; I knew I had never entered religious life. But I was paralyzed—*paralyzed*—with fear.

Many of you reading this are probably unable to imagine how any sane person could find themselves in such a mental and emotional state. Well, I have another surprise for you: There are *many, many other people* who are reading these words, nodding their heads, and saying, "I know *exactly* what he was going through." In fact, I was told that the "invalid marriage" obsession is an extremely common one among committed Christians with OCD.

Pastors, spiritual directors, and saints have long known about the phenomenon of scrupulosity. Christian psychiatrists now know that recurrent scrupulosity can be a symptom of OCD. For some people scruples are a passing trial on the road to conversion or to a deepening of their spiritual lives, and these are resolved by the time-honored method of obedience to a confessor or spiritual director. Chronic or recurrent scruples, however, may require treatment on another level.

In no way do I intend to reduce the value of spiritual direction here: For me there are three priests in particular whose wisdom and especially patience have saved me from utter darkness and confusion. My gratitude to God and to them will last forever. But an undeniable fact of OCD is that medications can bring relief to aspects of the problem that cannot be corrected in any other way. My daily life would be profoundly paralyzed and hindered if it were not for the medical treatment that I continue to receive for depression, OCD, and anxiety—this complex NID, this brain dysfunction that afflicts me. With regard to OCD, medication has reduced and even eliminated the intensity and strangeness of many obsessions. Medication alone doesn't work like magic, but it is an *essential* element in dealing with the problem.

In general, NIDs need to be treated as medical conditions. If you are suffering, don't let pride prevent you from acknowledging a mental illness. It will only get worse. It is right here that your spiritual freedom comes into play: *Get help.*

If you break your leg, you have to go to the doctor, undergo various treatments, and follow a therapeutic plan for recovery. Otherwise you won't be able to walk. If something is "broken" in the deeply complicated but still *physical* regions of the brain, you have to go to the doctor, undergo various treatments, and follow a therapeutic plan for recovery. The brain is the necessary instrument in God's plan for the expression and development of our integrally human capacities of knowledge and love. If it's not working right, you won't be able to think straight about yourself, your responsibilities, or your relationships.

I want to say something to priests and others involved in pastoral care: As shepherds, you care about all the needs of those entrusted to you. If some were hungry, you would feed them. I pray that you will learn as much as you need to about these psychiatric conditions, so that you can at least recognize signs of them in people who seek your help. Please try to establish referral links and relationships with competent and responsible people in the mental health profession. Encourage and foster the efforts of Christians in mental health care. You remain the indispensable instruments of God's grace, but you may also be able to direct people to sources of healing that will bring stability to their daily lives.

And I want to tell intelligent young Christian men and women, if God is calling you to a healing profession, please prayerfully consider psychiatric medicine or psychology. We need many more Christians practicing the mental health professions in the light of the gospel. We know that Jesus made the blind see and the deaf hear. But who knows how many of the multitudes were healed in their brains and emotions and freed from a lifetime of inner disability? Jesus needs you to be his healing hands in these most delicate places, where illness is so difficult to perceive.

People thus afflicted are all around us. And they usually don't look "weird" on the outside. They are not necessarily straightening picture frames all the time, hoarding old newspapers, sweating profusely, or staring at the ground with terror in their eyes. More often they seem just like you. They are your friends, colleagues, coworkers, neighbors, teachers, parents, children, husbands, or wives. And yes, they may be your priests, pastors, or leaders in the work of the Church.

These people laugh and joke; they are talented and capable in many ways; they may even be known for giving good advice to others; they may be some of the most admirable people you know. But they hurt terribly inside, and it is a great work of mercy to dedicate your life to binding up their wounds for the love of God. The Jesus who says, "I was sick and you visited me" (Matthew 25:36), is hidden in them, calling out to you.

CHAPTER SIX

A Prayer:
Crying Out in Pain From Body and Brain

Lord Jesus,
I am struck dumb,
immobile,
inside and outside.
My heart is shrouded by this misery;
my eyes, which look upon your holy face,
are stricken, assaulted by the light,
aching red, longing to be shut beneath their lids.

I have no voice
except an inner cry,
a mute, distressed animal whimper
that cannot even summon itself to ask for mercy.
My fingers drift
away from my hands,
and the tokens of your love
are beyond their reach.

How do I pray?
O Lord, where is the longing of my prayer?
Jesus, Mercy,

hear the struggle of breath;
Jesus, Mercy,
hear the scream inside
the shaken contours of this skull,
with brain pierced
by some fiery blade.

O God, Love!
Hear the endless noise,
the pounding,
the howling of skin and nerve,
muscle and joint:
this cacophony of pain
that groans all through the place
where I once felt that I had a body.

Jesus, Mercy, forgive me.
Jesus, Love.
Jesus, I offer.
I long for these to be my words to you,
but lips are speechless quiver,
and thought and heart are frozen in exhaustion.
Prayer is ice that does not flow.
Prayer is a voice of distant memory;
it feels like a stiff corpse
beneath my soul's total turmoil.
In the end there is nothing
but the hollowness that holds a thing called me
wanting you.
I want you, Jesus.

PART TWO

Suffering Day by Day

CHAPTER SEVEN

Wake Up

When we awaken each morning, let us offer our first thoughts to God.

Morning. Dreams fade. It's me. Me!

I wake up with the natural rush of morning, followed by the smack of consciousness telling me that *my* morning serves no purpose. And then that creepy exhaustion starts crawling through my limbs.

Oh, why is it me? How ugly and hateful a thing I am! I once knew who I was, didn't I? Then came the pain in the chest and shoulders, the heavy, aching head, the legs that drag, the anger and the exhaustion, the dullness, and the fear.

I was a college professor: I had students, classes, colleagues, my office, my school! But pain ate away at me. I struggled, but I lost my grip. I had to give up my job and go on disability. Now I teach in my dreams and wake up to the horror: "I've lost my job. I have spent my whole adult life preparing for this and doing this and thinking of myself as 'Professor Janaro,' and now it's gone!"

And an evil voice whispers inside my mental ear, "You are a failure. You are useless. You can't provide for your family. You have no place in the world." Who is saying that?

I am no longer who I was. Is that really true?

I have no place to go today. And the day's pain hasn't really kicked in. Sit up. Assume some attitude of prayer. I shall collect myself before God.

I sit in a mind fog, like the darkness and void of the first day of Creation. Except I am slipping back into the void. Where is the light?

I need my medications. I take the ones prescribed for the beginning of the day. I get out of bed and stumble to the bathroom. Then back to bed, back to sleep.

An hour and a half later, my eyes open again, and with a burst of cynical frustration (or is it resignation?) I grab my second prescribed dose of medication. I glance at the clock: Yes, it's time for *this* one. As I down the pills, I whisper, "Jesus," hoping that God will find a prayer in all of this.

Now I will say my prayers. I stubbornly pronounce the words. I know they mean something. Prayer is hard enough for healthy people. Jesus spoke about faith that moves mountains. The mountains right now are the sludge in my mind that hangs all over every word of prayer. My "usual" prayers—ugh! I drift from the Morning Offering. Where am I?

At what depth of immobility do I find my sunken heart? Is it there? Is it that inner "Arrrgh"? Is this sick and bitter thing my heart?

I look at Jesus on the cross. "Jesus, I don't want to be like this. I keep asking you to take this away, and you won't!" I am arguing with Jesus. It's a start. I keep talking. I listen. Then I lie back down and look at him and breathe. I don't know what I am trying to say to him. I am dozing again.

Sit up! Time for the Morning Offering. Yes, Lord, I offer you everything. Although, if it is compatible with your holy will, can you please make things better? Can you give me a break?

I take up Morning Prayer. The Psalms sometimes speak in a very personal way.

> To my words give ear, O Lord.
> Give heed to my groaning
> Attend to the sound of my cries,
> my King and my God. (Psalm 5:2, *NAB*)

Yes, Lord, you can hear my whole body groaning and my humiliated and sorrowful soul groaning. Forgive my bitterness, for I am a sinner, and I don't know how to bear anything in life. Look at me, Lord; look at my wounds, and see therein something that cries out to you.

Then there is an antiphon from Isaiah:

> You are a refuge to the poor, a refuge to the needy in distress;
> Shelter from the rain, shade from the heat. (Isaiah 25:4, *NAB*)

I am quiet. Am I truly "needy in distress," or am I the rich (but no longer so young) man who doesn't want to follow Jesus because Jesus has begun to take away a few of my possessions (see Matthew 19:16–22)? Both. Two attitudes struggle within me, slugging it out.

Jesus, don't let me turn away from you. Don't let me go away sad.

CHAPTER EIGHT

My Day?

So what am I going to do today?

I don't know if many healthy folks have any idea how gaping this question is for sick people. Some days I feel as if I want to die, but I can't. I have to live every nasty moment.

Everything hurts. Everything is degrading. My consciousness is dominated by various physical dysfunctions, and I mark time.

How can chronic pain be described?

Sometimes it is tolerable. I might have "a pretty good day." Sometimes it is tolerable only with pain medication. Other times, forget it—I ache everywhere: the neck and shoulders; the thighs and knees are the worst; but every muscle and every joint and, it seems, every organic tissue of my body hurts, starting at the top of my head. My skin hurts. My eyes are sore. All the way down my body, bone and tissue and muscle, each sounds its individual note in a symphony of aches. My shins hurt. The soles of my feet hurt. The little joints in my toes *hurt!* All I want to do is lie flat on my back. Unfortunately, my back hurts.

I am too exhausted to do anything. I can't read. I can't write. I can't think. Just being alive is like heavy work. I can't rest. I don't know where to put my arms and legs. Why don't they just float away? Where does affliction end and discouragement begin? The most difficult thing is the fear that this is all my fault.

Maybe there is a TV program that will distract me for an hour. But sometimes I have so much light and noise sensitivity that I can't stand to have the thing on even when the program is interesting. I have some thoughts about television and illness, but I'll save them for later.

I have to justify breathing the world's air by making a *contribution*. My poor wife is tired of doing all the things that I can't do. My children need the example of a father who is firm, dedicated, devoted, and engaged with the world and with the well-being of his family. And I just lie here like a stone. "Daddy is sick"—we all know that. Or has he just given up? Lord, don't let me give up!

I am the stone. The stone has been taken away from the tomb. Who could have moved such a stone? And he is not there: "They have taken away my Lord, and I do not know where they have laid him" (John 20:13).

He is risen!

CHAPTER NINE

God's Day

The truth is that the first person I encounter every morning when I open my eyes is God. Everything around me is God's creation, through which he greets me. I breathe in his air and open my eyes to his light. The day rushes at me, with all its hopes and its trials, out of which he will build the road that will lead me on my journey. The amazing thing is that even on the worst of days I can still remember that this is true.

Offering my life to God first thing in the morning is a way of acknowledging with gratitude that my being, my life, and everything I have belong to him. I am *who* I am because I am *his creature*. Everything that is "me" is the effect, here and now, of his direct and personal creative and sustaining love. This is what matters, even without professional honors, or a job, or the ability to do much of anything. His love is everything. Outside of that love there is nothing—not even ashes.

I give thanks to the Lord that he has grounded my life in his truth. Suffering can drive me to forget or to lose focus. But reality remains what it is, and Jesus holds on to me inside that reality and enables me to remember it. He does this through the mystery of his Church, his people who for two thousand years have risen each morning and offered their prayers to God.

And so when I wake up, in whatever condition, with whatever misery or whatever happy expectation, the truth is that I am not alone. I am invited to pray in union with the whole people of God, with the angels and saints, with every creature that exists to sing his praise.

A Short Morning Offering
My God, I love you.
I am in your hand.
Take my life,
and make me what you will me to be.

A Meditation on the Morning Offering
Most Sacred Heart of Jesus,
who loves us so much,
you have revealed the Father's mercy,
    which seeks the heart of every human person:
    "For God so loved the world that he gave his only-begotten
        Son,
    that whoever believes in him should not perish
    but have eternal life" (John 3:16).
I believe in your love for me, and I beg you:
Lord Jesus, have mercy on me, a sinner.
I thank you for the gift of your infinite mercy:
the blood and water pouring forth from your heart,
    which takes away my sins,
    which takes away the sins of the world.

Jesus, I love you.
Jesus, I trust in you.

I offer you this poor little day:
I offer you
　my thoughts,
　　words,
　　and actions,
　　　that by the transforming power of your love
　　my littleness might give you glory
　　and become a sign of your beauty
　　and of the particular, saving love you bear for every person
I meet today.

I offer you my sufferings,
　　　that by your grace I might embrace them in faith and love
　　　and bear them in patience, serenity, and Christian hope;
　　so that through them your Holy Spirit might lead me
　　along the secret paths of your compassion,
　　using my pain, weakness, and sorrows
　　as instruments of solidarity and saving strength
　　toward those unknown to whom you seek to touch
in your unfathomable mercy.

I offer you everything
in union with the holy Mother of God,
the Immaculate Heart of Mary,
mother of tenderness and mercy,
she who is close to all who labor
and all who suffer.
And I ask you to renew me by the power of your Spirit,

that I might cry out, "Abba, Father,"
sustained by the radiance of your countenance
and the ineffable splendor of your crucified heart,
O Jesus, Lover of Mankind.

A Fool's Morning Prayer

O Lord, my God,
you can do all things.
By your ineffable power
and for the sake of your incalculable,
magnanimous, steadfast love,
for the glory of your divine patience
and inexhaustible mercy,
make me
a little less stupid, vain, negligent,
hypocritical, envious, spiteful,
covetous, picky, lazy, complaining,
distracted, self-pitying, unforgiving
today than I was yesterday.
Amen.

CHAPTER TEN

A Reflection: I Want to Go Outside

It is a beautiful, early spring afternoon.
It is warm, and the sun is shining.
I want to go outside.
I love the gentle sun
and the wind
and the trees still bare but ready to blossom.
I want to go outside.

Why don't I go outside?
Why, O Lord?
I could take a walk today.
I don't have much pain.
Or I could just sit in a chair
and watch my children play.
Why don't I go outside?

Am I too lazy to go outside?
Maybe that is it.

That is what I worry about.
Worrying is a lot of work.
I am not too lazy to worry about being lazy,
but sometimes it makes me tired.
When I am too tired to worry,
I stop and I sleep.
I worry and I sleep.

Why don't I go outside?
Please let me go outside;
But I do not go.

My daughter wants me
to come outside
and watch her ride her bike.
So I go out,
and I smile,
and I say, "Very good, Teresa."

Now I am outside in the yard,
but I am still inside.
The inside goes wherever I go.
But it is not so bad.
I am glad for my little girl.

There was a time
when watching the children
was like watching a video
of people I once knew,
in the days when I used to be alive.
Now Teresa can touch me,
and I can feel a little bit of sun.

And I remember
that it is good for me to be here.

O God, you are good.
I love you.
Have mercy on me.
I am inside, and so are you.
I am tired,
very tired.
I will sleep now
and worry a little less.

CHAPTER ELEVEN

In the Hands of God

From the bed to the bathroom. From the bathroom to the chair. Try to read. I am tired. From the chair to the bed. A little music and a nap. Back to the chair for more reading.

The kids are running about, playing, prattling, fighting, annoying me to death. My wife is in and out, on her feet, doing things like a normal person. For me it's another day in "the cage." I feel frustrated. I hate it. Well, no one ever said I had to like it. Yet God is at work in me. The day is not wasted. How do I know this?

I am not going to pretend that I suffer cheerfully. I am not there yet. Or at least I don't feel very cheerful. I am struggling. But I know that my suffering has meaning. I know that Jesus embraces me through it. I pray that I will grow in the awareness of these realities. I am trying, and I am praying for God's grace. But I know it will take time.

Knowing that my suffering has meaning is in itself something that amazes me. Even more, it astounds me to know that it is even *possible* to be cheerful and to have profound peace in the midst of great sufferings. I did not arrive at this knowledge from the natural world. Where did it come from?

I belong to a people—God's people, the Church—where there are witnesses to this great peace and cheerful acceptance of suffering, not only the saints but even some people I know (and what a blessing those people are to me). It is *faith* that enables me to recognize this and to know that it is really true.

I know that the beginning of this peace is to be aware of God's presence and his plan for my life. The road to a peaceful and cheerful acceptance of God's plan passes through the practice of patience and trust. "Jesus, I trust in you" begins as a prayer—a prayer that in a certain sense says, "Jesus I am afraid. I do not know how to trust. Give me the grace to trust in you."

The practice of this prayer develops into a habit, and out of this habitual prayer God forms in us and with us (slowly) the Christian virtues, especially humility and courage. And so I pray to grow more actively aware of the truth that God's mercy defines my life.

To be honest, I do not know how much I *understand* all this concretely. I could write a book on the theology of suffering, but how much do I really understand in a vital way? I see it through a dark glass, a very dark glass. So I pray. I offer everything to God in the morning. Then I grunt through the day, feeling lousy and barking at my loved ones. (Perhaps I am not that bad; you will have to ask my wife if you really want to know.) Then at night I examine the worst of the day's mess, make the act of contrition, and really mean it.

But the next day is pretty much the same. Will I ever grow beyond this level? I pray that God may sustain *hope* in my heart. I know that God's grace can make something out of my nothingness, and therefore I must not—*I will not*—be discouraged.

My trials have opened my eyes, my ears, and my heart to something I never noticed in my youth. Maybe it is because I have finally started listening to people. The fact is that many people are suffering, many of them more than I. Indeed, suffering is deeper than the immediate external struggles that engage most of us. Everyone has something missing in life, something that has disappointed, something that does not measure up to a once-cherished hope, something that inhibits freedom, some burden that tires, some hunger that is never satisfied.

People usually accommodate themselves to reduced expectations about life, especially as they get older. How else could they get through the day? Sometimes, however, one can still catch an echo of a cry of pain, that deep and mysterious pain at the heart of every human life. Life is, in some measure, always something that has to be endured.

Why is this? We suffer because of sin: original sin, our own personal sins, and the sins of the world. We suffer in Christ, who is God's love made personal and particular for each one of us. Jesus is God drawn close to our wounded humanity, so close that he takes it upon himself—not merely in some general way but in a way that encompasses each one of us.

Jesus is the intimate companion of each and every human person, even those who do not know him. He knows each one of us; God the eternal Son of the Father unites himself to my humanity and to your humanity. He lives in us and suffers in us and through us. He accompanies us through our companionship with one another and reaches out to others through our witness.

Jesus knows who I am and who he wills me to be. He knows the secret of why I was created. He knows my sins. He knows how to heal me of them, how to draw me to himself, how to make me the adopted son that I am meant to be in him for all eternity.

And so my joys and sufferings are his infinitely wise, uniquely crafted, and tender love through which he shapes my life and leads me to my destiny. How little I really understand about my destiny. How little I understand about the eternal life that means belonging to him forever.

We must remember every day that God is with us and that he draws us toward our true identity, which is to reflect his eternal glory in that unique way that is ours. Each of us is a person created in his image and likeness—a reflection that we do not yet understand but that he sees and knows. We ought to call this frequently to mind and dwell on it.

Those little prayers throughout the day are worth so much: "Jesus, I love you. Jesus, I trust in you. Come, Holy Spirit." No matter the storms and the fury, the depths of our lives are not solitude. At the heart of life, of every moment of life, is companionship with the merciful God. He is "on the other side" of our prayers—listening, full of tender love, wanting to bestow mercy on us at every moment, with an attentiveness and care infinitely greater than that of any father or mother for his or her children.

We must remind ourselves of this in the course of our day. We are Christians. We believe in the Trinity, the Incarnation, good and evil, judgment, heaven, and hell. We believe that

Jesus died on the cross for us. Yet it is so, so easy to fall into a pattern of life that misses the point of all of this. We can begin to think, "God is in heaven, and it is only after death that we are really going to meet him and have to deal with him. He has accomplished his plan, our redemption. He has set up his rules, and we had better make sure we keep them. As for the rest, there is me and my life, a sort of self-contained little universe, which—as long as it stays within God's rules—is basically mine to do with as I wish."

What children we are! Sometimes we act as if religion is sort of like school. It takes up a fixed part of our time; it is somehow necessary for our future life, although we have little idea why; in spite of the fact that it is generally boring, we enjoy it every once in a while, but basically we cannot wait until its requirements are over and we can get on to what really interests us for the day—playtime! My time for *me*! As Venerable John Henry Newman once said, "[T]he aim of most men esteemed conscientious and religious…is, to all appearance, not how to please God, but how to please themselves without displeasing Him."[1]

It is easy to get into a routine of daily religious duties, trying not to break the commandments, and then—with the rest of our time (that is, *most* of our time)—look out for ourselves, doing what we want to do, trying to make a good life for ourselves. It is not surprising that when suffering afflicts us, we feel like children forced to do chores. Whatever its form, suffering feels like something outside the normal course of life, an invasion of "my life." I am stuck with this while others are allowed to go on playing.

Our hearts long for happiness and are drawn by the goodness and beauty of reality. Is the promise of happiness that reality holds out to us a lie? Have we been betrayed by existence?

This is the great temptation: to despair of any fulfillment to the longing and the hope of the human heart; to be convinced that the universe is a trick and that the heart must be suffocated—or at least distracted until it is finally swallowed up by death and ceases to torment us.

With our faith and hope for a fuller life to come, we Christians may be tempted to go through the motions of resignation while nourishing a secret bitterness that we have been cheated out of any possibility of satisfying the longing of our hearts. We may feel that we can only "pass time," reconciling ourselves to mediocrity and misery in a world where God is absent, looking vaguely toward a future life. While such an attitude is better than despair, if this is as far as we go in enduring suffering, our relationship with God will remain narrow and constrained.

This is not reality. It is not only an immature way of living our faith; it is ultimately based on a kind of *practical* illusion: We know the *idea* that God loves us and cares for us every moment of our lives, but how deeply has that penetrated our hearts?

This realization should not lead us to condemn ourselves for being such immature Christians. God is good and merciful; he works with whatever feeble adherence we offer him. Let us beg him to deepen our faith, hope, and love. The only mature Christian is a dead Christian. By this, of course, I mean a Christian judged, fully purged of his or her sinfulness, and beholding the face of God. While we live we are still growing.

Growing can be painful and incomprehensible. But there is Someone in our lives *all* the time, shaping every moment, designing our days so as to lead us to him. I do not have the capacity to imagine what his design is for me, just as a child does not have the capacity to imagine what it will be like to be an adult. Let us ask God to show us how we really are growing.

Each of us has our own suffering, and there is really no sense in complaining that I am suffering more than someone else. First of all, I do not really know that. Second, I am suffering what God knows I need to in order for me to become the person he has created me to be.

The fact remains that we struggle with suffering. There is the irreducible *sting*, the day-to-day, step-by-step endurance of it all. God, who loves us, and who himself has experienced the mystery of suffering, does not take lightly our cries of pain or our feeling that there is something wrong with it all, that it shouldn't be this way, that we are wounded.

I have cried out to God, "Why, O Lord, did you put me in a world full of persons and things that are good and beautiful and fill me with aspirations to accomplish things—good things, things that would give you glory? Why did you sow these desires in my heart and then let me fall into this cage? Why must I endure this debility when my heart yearns not to do evil but to embrace the good and affirm your glory?"

The answer to this question could be expressed in everything I have said above. Yet I think that the experience of suffering challenges us to go one step further if our hearts are to begin to learn that God really loves us here and now, personally and completely, that he loves the whole of us, and that this life is not just a game.

In reality created things *are* good. Life is good. My life is good. Jesus knew this: No man has ever known so profoundly what a marvelous and wonderful thing it is to live! If all we say about suffering is, "I guess I have to have it bad now so that I can have it good in heaven," I do not think we have said enough. The human heart is not satisfied with this. When Jesus said in the garden, "Father, if you are willing, remove this chalice from me" (Luke 22:42), he was speaking from the very depths of his sacred humanity. He was affirming the fundamental perception that it is good to live, to be treated with justice, kindness, and dignity, to flourish as a human being. The physical and earthly needs of the human person and human society are a concern of the Church because they, too, are the object of God's mercy.

God wants to comfort us in our afflictions and console us in our sorrows, but above all he wants to teach our hearts that he is with us always. He wants to open our hearts to the experience of something that we cannot perceive by ourselves: that the realities of our daily life mean *more*—not less—than we understand.

Suffering must be endured not because life is less important than we had hoped but because it is *more important than we can imagine*. It is the place where *God is with us*.

Our hearts long for happiness, for life. But what is life? What is happiness? Do we find it only in that space of time that belongs to us? Do we imagine that God sits in the background and allows us to play with reality, then starts taking our toys away when playtime is over? No! This is not what life is! Life is *God with us* at every moment—in every joy (God delights in our joy!) and also in the abyss.

"Father, into your hands I commit my spirit!" (Luke 23:46). This, too, is the expression of the human heart of Jesus, and it is the supreme affirmation of the value of *everything* in life. In our trials we may not *feel* the presence of God, but in our endurance and in our prayer (even our most inarticulate and desperate prayer), he is leading us to the truth that every moment has value because he is with us. And so we must open our hearts to him and allow him to shape us according to the mystery of his love. We must pray in faith and hope that we might love God, who embraces us within the life he has given us.

God knows how hard it is to suffer. But he has created us to love. Our hearts are made for him. We can only grow in this life by recognizing him and loving him more.

Do I feel as if I cannot love him more? Do I want him to draw away, at least a little, and give me back some of my space? Of course I feel that way, but I must *pray* and *beg* him to teach me to love him more, because his presence and his love are real.

We are called to endure suffering not with stoic resignation but with abandonment to his loving presence. We endure in the conviction that God offers us his love—the only fulfillment of the human heart—*here and now*, in the midst of our sufferings and the plodding of our daily lives. We are called to put our hearts on the line, to allow ourselves to be wounded by the hope that even in this darkness it is possible to love and to be loved, because he is with us and he loves us *now*. And we know that love—in the end—is always worth the risk.

The abyss is the hollow of the hands of God.

Jesus spent a significant portion of his public ministry healing people. It is true that the healing of the body is a symbol of the healing of the person from sin. And it is also true that the miracles of healing demonstrated his divine power. But I am always touched by the particular indications in the Gospels that he "had compassion for them" (Matthew 9:36, 14:14; Mark 6:34, 8:2).

Jesus came to save us from our sins. He came to save us through love. And that divine and human love burned with compassion for all the fragility of our afflictions, our sickness, and our poverty.

And we all suffer from the "sickness" of mortality, the fruit of the sin of Adam. Every one of us will die, and none of us will find it easy. Remember, at the moment of your death, that you are passing through the hands of God's compassion.

CHAPTER TWELVE

Praying the Promise

Hope Does Not Disappoint (A Meditation on Romans 5)
Lord Jesus Christ,
you have united us to the mystery
of your death and resurrection.
Through you "we have obtained access
to this grace in which we stand,
and we rejoice in our hope of sharing the glory of God."

Lord Jesus,
make us steadfast in trials;
indeed, enable us to "*rejoice* in our sufferings,
knowing that suffering produces endurance,
and endurance produces character,
and character produces hope,
and hope does not disappoint us,
because God's love has been poured
into our hearts
through the Holy Spirit
who has been given to us."
Grant us in ever greater abundance

the grace of your Spirit,
so that—as "once sin reigned in death"
over the whole human race—
"grace also might reign through righteousness
to eternal life through [you],
Jesus Christ our Lord."

Who Shall Separate Us From the Love of Christ?
  (A Meditation on Romans 8)
Lead us, O Spirit of God,
that we might be children of God.
Drive away the spirit of slavery,
lest we fall back into fear,
and empower us with the spirit of sonship.
Place within us the cry, "Abba! Father!"
that we might be children of God:
children and therefore heirs,
"heirs of God and fellow heirs with Christ"—
lifted up by his saving death
and thus called to suffer with him
in order that we may also be glorified with him.
Let us love God, who in everything works for our good.
Let us live in the hope of the glory to be revealed.
For thus nothing will separate us from the love of Christ.

"Who shall separate us from the love of Christ?"
No trial of this life will be able to separate us from the love of
God
  in Christ Jesus our Lord.
No fallen angels or principalities will be able to separate us
from the love of God
  in Christ Jesus our Lord.

No powers of this world will be able to separate us from the
love of God
    in Christ Jesus our Lord.
No tribulation will be able to separate us from the love of God
    in Christ Jesus our Lord.
No distress will be able to separate us from the love of God
    in Christ Jesus our Lord.
No persecution will be able to separate us from the love of
God
    in Christ Jesus our Lord.
No famine will be able to separate us from the love of God
    in Christ Jesus our Lord.
No nakedness, or peril, or sword will be able to separate us
from the love of God
    in Christ Jesus our Lord.

Even if they kill us all the day long, they will not be able to separate us
from the love of God in Christ Jesus our Lord.
Even if we are regarded as sheep to be slaughtered, they will
not be able to separate us
from the love of God in Christ Jesus our Lord.
Death will not be able to separate us
from the love of God in Christ Jesus our Lord.
The fear of death will not be able to separate us
from the love of God in Christ Jesus our Lord.

"No, in all these things we are more than conquerors through
him who loved us."
Jesus has loved us.
Jesus loves us.

CHAPTER THIRTEEN

A Sack of Potatoes Needs You

How do I feel today? Rejected.

Oh, I know it isn't true. I know that God loves me and that my family and friends love me. I am surrounded by people who love me. Why do I feel rejected?

Pain and a sense of uselessness. The world goes on, just as it does every day, and I feel entirely superfluous. I know it's not true. I am a husband and a father, and I am a writer trying to articulate this struggle so that others can understand or perhaps feel that they themselves are understood. But I feel like a sack of potatoes.

Do I need a bit of good old-fashioned cheering up? For all that I have said about depression as a disease, cheering up certainly does not do any harm. But on some of these days, cheering up can be at best a temporary patch. I must be prepared to deal with the possibility that today might just be a washout.

Nevertheless, I want to tell the healthy and able people of the world: Do not underestimate the value of the *time* you spend with someone who is suffering. You are afraid because you can't solve the person's problems. Of course you can't. So don't pressure yourself. Give your time. Stay with the person, and be consistent about it. In human things time and presence are the media of love.

If the person turns his face to the wall and grunts, that doesn't mean you should go away. The person may not want to talk, and it is not your responsibility to entertain. If when you leave he is sulking, you have not failed. Come again. Bring something of your own to do. It is love to stay with another person, even while you clean out your purse or go through your wallet or read a magazine. But don't go away! Stay with the person.

So how do I feel now after writing that paragraph? I still feel like a sack of potatoes.

Permit me a brief digression here. I must say that television is better than nothing, especially when a person is in physical pain. There are many times when I have thanked God for the TV. I do not have the energy or the patience to learn those complex relaxation and meditation techniques recommended for chronic pain. TV, however, can distract me from pain up to a point.

But distraction is not a strategy for life. And watching TV alone, all the time, is a sad thing. On the Day of Judgment, Jesus is not going to say, "Blessed are you. When I was sick, you turned on the TV and left the room."

This is not a criticism of hospitals or health professionals. I know they are overextended. I have seen their great dedication, both in my own hospital stays and in the tremendous efforts made on behalf of my daughter. Rather, this is a lament about the loneliness in our world. When you are sick, and all you have for a companion is a remote, something seems missing. You lie there glassy-eyed and drooling and someone turns on the TV for you, gives some kick to the volume, and walks away with a cheery smile.

Televisions blare like noisy animals in the houses of the sick. I wonder how desolate it must be for some poor forgotten person in a long-term care facility to be trapped in a frozen body with the TV yapping away all day. I pray that more good souls will experience the call of God to an apostolate of simple human presence. This is a courageous work of mercy.

Still, I understand the blaring televisions and the impetus of mercy behind them. We are confused: We do not know the love of God, and we feel helpless in front of suffering. We live in a problem-solving society, and we can't solve the problem of suffering. So we present the suffering person with a TV, which makes human noises. It is a feeble way of saying, "We are still here with you." (After all, no one puts on the TV for corpses in a mortuary.) We know this is a person. We know this person deserves love. We want to be present; we want to love somehow.

This TV noise is how we express love to each other. Small and cold this love, but still it is love. There is hope, a pinpoint of love light, a distant star.

Let me tie in this digression about TV with my main point. I think that one of the important things we need to learn in the world today is that there are layers of human suffering that cannot be "fixed." The only way to touch a person at this level of their pain is with love, simple love. And this kind of love requires *time*.

If you spend a few hours with a sack of potatoes, it will still be a sack of potatoes when you leave. But don't think you have wasted your time; you have to keep coming back—every day or week or whatever you can give. If the person acts grouchy and doesn't seem to appreciate your being around, don't go away, and don't stop coming. Don't try too hard to be helpful or make the person feel good. Just be familiar, be natural, and be there.

If the sack of potatoes is someone you like, you might start to enjoy spending time with him or her. You will find things to do, to talk about, and to learn. This is good. But don't depend on this. Pain makes for a fickle friend, unfortunately. You must give the time as a sacrifice and expect nothing in return.

This means that you are often going to feel awkward. You are going to feel that you are not in control and, for the most part, you are going to feel unappreciated. But this is good. It means you have begun to enter into and to share the burden of the awful loneliness and intolerable dullness that are at the heart of another person's pain.

Forgive me if I make what might seem to be an impertinent statement: People who are blessed with good health and emotional stability need to make *more* sacrifices. There are many ways to help those in need. By all means use your energy to assist with the many practical difficulties that sick and suffering people (and their families) must endure. But please do not forget that deeper and harder sacrifice of sharing time with the person in pain. Simple love passes through time, patience, and perseverance and entails the willingness not merely to help but to suffer with the person.

CHAPTER FOURTEEN

Prayers in Sickness and Distress

Nothing Without You

O God, O Jesus, O vivifying Spirit,
without you I can do nothing.

Without you
every moment is a crushing burden,
every trial pricks and stings
    my tired flesh,
and every person is set against me,
    opposing me with abuse,
    chilling me with icy indifference,
    sickening me with rehearsed consolations,
    or boring me with the tedious diligence
        of their love,
        their concern,
        their sincere, small hearts,
        in which they struggle to sustain me
        but cannot hold me

because I have become
so distant and so enormous in my misery.

Without you
I do nothing;
I am nothing;
I am a huge, hollow hole of nothing.

O Lord, my God;
O Jesus, Redeemer and Healer;
O Holy Spirit, Lord and Giver of Life:
with you
I can do all
   that lies at hand
   in the small space of today.
With you
I can endure anything
   that your wisdom and love lay upon me.
I can endure
   your yoke, placed so tenderly
   upon my sore skin;
   your burden light,
      lifting me in breezes of heaven.

With you
every person has a place
   inside the freedom you create in me.
And those who love me,
   those who carry me,
   are great in their humble hearts,
   which give me the joy of your healing touch.

A Meditation on Being Loved
Dear Lord,
thank you for the love
of the many good people
who support,
encourage,
and assist me.
Their love is beautiful
in its many facets
and modes of expression.
There is love
in gestures and actions
and self-sacrifice—
so many ways to love
that I never would have recognized
if I were not so needy.

But it is not enough, O Lord.
It is never enough.
The love of people,
all the generosity of their hearts,
is frail and small
and falls short,
and I still feel alone.
The core of me still calls out,
listening for an answering voice.
All the love of the world
would still leave me empty
without you.
I might never have known this
if I were not so needy.

Lord, love me;
please love me.
I believe in your love for me,
even when I do not feel it.
Give me the grace to trust in your love for me
and to recognize your love
in the good human hands held out to me.

CHAPTER FIFTEEN

God's People, My People

There are times when I have to let myself be carried by those who love me. I cannot trust my own judgment. I know that the way in which I perceive myself is distorted.

There are people God has placed in my life through whom Jesus looks at me and communicates his love—his concrete affirmation of the value of who I am—in circumstances where I simply cannot see it myself. These people are my family, my friends who really know me, and, in a singular way, my wife.

No, they do not fully understand me, nor is their love for me perfect. I am tempted to distance myself from them because of these imperfections and to hold stubbornly to my own isolation. But then I recall that it is Jesus who enters my situation and my confusion and my self-doubts through these persons.

With my wife there is that great mystery—the sacrament of marriage. Husbands and wives always have different perceptions and personalities; they inevitably disappoint one another, fail to satisfy one another's need for affection; their attention to one another and support for one another are weak. There are so many excuses for drifting apart, because we forget about the sacrament. But Jesus is present in a unique way in this relationship. He entrusts two people to each other, and he has determined that this fragile human companionship be the instrument of his saving love.

In times of desperation I have cried out to God and have discovered in my wife the strength without which I could not survive. It is not that she is a mystic, or a great saint, or a brilliant doctor, or even that she understands what I am going through. But she sees my suffering, prays to the Lord, and loves me as best she can. Jesus is there giving his power to her love for me and transforming my own suffering into his mysterious gift to her, leading her closer to him. This is not always apparent to either one of us in times of trial, but when we look back at what we have endured together, we can see that it is true.

So this must be our prayer: to draw upon this truth and this power from Christ more and more, to let it form every day, every moment. This is the real mystical grace of the sacrament of marriage. If they remember Christ at the center of the relationship, husband and wife will be led to God.

Marriage is a special kind of companionship, but friendships in Christ are a source of great strength as well. Some people are not called to marriage, but all are called to friendship, to experience the love of Christ in the Church, his people. Friendships are, after all, founded on the sacrament of baptism. I cannot live without my friends. What happens among us is an event on the path to salvation, because Jesus has put us together. He can use everything about us—even our faults—provided we seek him and recognize him.

When we forget Jesus, our friendships become dissipated or false. We hide from each other, flatter each other, nourish secret grievances, and eventually begin to fight. Suffering is one way that Jesus reminds us that we need him and each other. And that makes me grateful for my own suffering.

What I say here about marriage and friendship is not just true for sick people or depressed people: It is true for everyone. God does not want anyone to be alone. He does not want you to be alone. Believe this, and pray about this, and never give up believing and praying and searching for that love. It is God's promise, and God always keeps his promises. Trust him. Allow Jesus to shape your loneliness into prayer.

CHAPTER SIXTEEN

The Lament

The saints tell us that we must bear suffering patiently. We must resist the temptation to grumble against God.

In a way faith intensifies this temptation, because we know in faith that God allows us to endure pain and suffering in order to purify us, lead us to him, and participate in his redeeming love for others. We are tempted to reject his will for us or rather to *resent* his will for us. As we know from human experience, resentment poisons a personal relationship. It will do violence to our relationship with God.

I know this temptation. I know it especially when I am tempted to envy people who prosper while I am afflicted. Often, however, I find a hidden blessing in my own illness: I am too exhausted to be angry, envious, or resentful of God or anyone else. The hardest times are when I am feeling a bit better but know it is not going to last. When I start to feel worse again, I am tempted to grumble, "It's not fair!"

So is that what I want: fairness? Another word for *fairness* is *justice*. If I demand justice, I will probably discover that I do not deserve much consideration. In fact, I am suffering a great deal less than I deserve. If life were merely fair, we would be doomed.

God's love and mercy are not fair; they are beyond measure. They are as wide as the freedom of God himself. OK, I will drop the "fairness" thing.

But still I hurt. The throbbing, pinching, pounding of dumb animal pain goes on day in and day out; it refuses to listen to spiritual direction and knows nothing about theology. These words I write grope their way through the mists of brain fog. I write for two days and then collapse for the next three. As you read this, realize that between one paragraph and the next there may be hours or even days of mostly lying in bed or limiting myself to simple activities. Really, writing this book exhausts me. *Why, O Lord?*

Am I grumbling?

I think it is important to distinguish between the grumble and the lament. Both can express themselves as "God, why are you doing this to me?" But they mean two different things. The lament is a prayer; read the Psalms. It is a cry of pain—the pain that a creature feels under the weight of the transforming pressure of the divine Creator and Lover, who carries out his mysterious plan in my life via an incomprehensible suffering. The grumble, on the other hand, is a loss of trust in God motivated by my own misery. It gets me forty more years in the desert—read the book of Exodus.

The Israelites grumbled against the Lord in the desert not just because they were hungry and thirsty but because this suffering made them forget all the signs and wonders of the loving God, who had delivered them from slavery and had proven his faithfulness over and over again. Instead of asking God to give them food and drink, they said, "Why did we ever leave Egypt?"

Still, what does God do in his enduring mercy for his people? He feeds them with manna from heaven. He quenches their thirst with water from the rock. God is so wonderful. He is so good. How can we not love him?

But it did not take long for the Israelites to start complaining that the manna was a monotonous diet. "In Egypt we had meat!" This is the path of grumbling. It leads away from God's love and into selfishness and ingratitude.

On the other hand, let us listen to the prophet Jeremiah: "Cursed be the day on which I was born!" (Jeremiah 20:14). He has just been beaten and put in stocks in front of the gates of the temple for public humiliation, because he has prophesied the coming destruction of Jerusalem. Jeremiah constantly laments over the vocation that God has given him: to be the prophet of disaster and therefore the prophet whom everyone wants to persecute. "Why did I come forth from the womb to see toil and sorrow, and spend my days in shame?" (20:18). In his misery he seems to wish he had never been born. That sounds like grumbling, doesn't it?

But there is a difference. In the midst of this lament, Jeremiah also says, "O Lord of hosts, who test the righteous, who see the heart and the mind,... to you have I committed my cause" (20:12). Jeremiah does not understand his own suffering. He does not understand why he even exists. Why, O Lord, should a man be born to such misery? And yet he *trusts* in the

Lord and remains faithful to the mission that causes his suffering. This fidelity—and even the lament of poor human flesh grappling with divine mystery—leads him into the very heart of God's love.

Our relationship with God is mysterious, and its trials are part of the mystery. We are called to share in the infinite life and love of God, we flesh-and-blood human beings who have a hard time getting out of bed in the morning even on a good day. We are called by God to a relationship that is destined to transform us into his likeness, to "divinize" us. This is going to take some stretching, to say the least.

And on top of the simple fragility of human beings, we all have the effects of original sin and our own personal sins with which we must contend. Then there is the further mystery of the suffering that God calls us to endure for the sake of others in order to participate in his redemptive love (more on this later).

So we must suffer. Jesus has suffered for all of us, and he suffers in all of us. He is the reason why redemption and glory are destined to rise up out of our own suffering. We simply need to adhere to him in faith, hope, and love.

In the life of the Church, God has given us signs that suffering has indeed been transformed. Some saints have experienced the marvel of an ecstatic and wholly supernatural joy—a kind of anticipation of glory—that penetrates the heart of suffering. Such joy—the foretaste of glory—is a kind of miracle, a special gift of grace. It is given to chosen souls, through whom it lights the way for us all. We can see radical examples of this miracle of ecstasy and glory in the ancient accounts of the early Christian martyrs.

For example, the Church in Rome has long preserved the memory of what must have been a profound and mystical embrace of martyrdom by the young deacon Lawrence in the third century. The saint is said to have joked to his executioners as he was being roasted alive, "You can turn me over. I'm *done* on this side."

Today some say that this story is a legend, but the testimony of centuries of popular piety implies that Lawrence must have embraced his suffering with a truly miraculous exaltation. His joy is a sign for us, not unlike the Transfiguration was for Jesus' disciples. It is a flash of eternity in the memory of God's people, reminding them of the real truth of the things of time.

(In the spirit of this transcendent humor, the Christian people honor Saint Lawrence as the patron of *cooks*. This is not a crude parody but a recognition in the heart of the Church that the triumph of the cross penetrates all the way to the details of ordinary life.)

The exalted courage and superhuman endurance of the martyrs and other suffering saints are special graces given to chosen souls. Even more mysterious is the experience of spiritual darkness, through which many saints share in the mystery of the suffering of Jesus on the cross. The Lord gives this grace to those he has prepared for it.

I will not venture to speculate on the manner in which the sufferings of ordinary life are pierced by that mystical ray of luminous darkness. When I examine my own conscience, I am inclined to conclude that most of the darkness I experience is due to a weakness of faith, hope, and love—and of course, the disease of depression and the pain of Lyme disease. If there is anything more profound, it is the secret work of God, which I shall entrust to his wisdom.

I pray for light. I want to at least understand what is going on. But I know I need above all to pray for the grace to let God have his way in my life. So I pray for wisdom, understanding, knowledge, counsel, fortitude, piety, and the fear of the Lord (see Isaiah 11:2).

The Holy Spirit gives his gifts to every Christian, and through them we grow in the likeness of God, which is our vocation. Each one of us is called to become God-like—that is, our destiny is to participate in the life of God. We know that it is here that our ultimate happiness lies. But God alone knows what our true destiny really looks like. "No eye has seen, nor ear heard, nor the heart of man conceived, what God has prepared for those who love him" (2 Corinthians 2:9; see Isaiah 64:4). So we must let him lead the way.

I do not seek the dark night of the soul. Nor do I look for revelations and ecstasies. Indeed, I want to resist the temptation to analyze (and anticipate!) the path that God is laying out before me. I am a beginner. I pray to feel better, and when I suffer, I pray—when I remember—for the grace to allow God to accomplish his mysterious work in me. The grace and the gifts of the Holy Spirit are there, not overwhelming my emotions with instant joy but opening my heart to the signs of God's presence, with enough certainty and enough courage to take the next step.

We must not be discouraged, or even surprised, that we are not enraptured by unspeakable joys and the foretaste of glory in the midst of our trials. Peace, patience, and above all prayerful fidelity in suffering constitute the path most of us are called to travel. Perhaps we can manage to be cheerful in the midst of suffering; this is a courageous virtue and one not easily attained.

Mother Teresa counseled us to receive everything from God with a smile. She also acknowledged that sometimes it is hard to smile at Jesus.[1] Cheerfulness is a sign that we are growing in love, but growing takes time.

Mother Teresa also told a story of a little girl who was in great pain. Mother Teresa told her that the pain was Jesus kissing her. The girl replied, "Please ask Jesus not to kiss me so much."[2]

There is no sin in this response. There is no sin in saying, "I hurt. This hurts. Why, O Lord, why must I hurt like this?" This is a form of prayer called the "lament." The Psalms are eloquent in expressing this profound human experience.

To accept God's will in suffering, it is not necessary to pretend that we don't hurt. Nor is it necessary to pretend that, because we embrace God's will, the pain doesn't bother us. Nor is it necessary to pretend that we understand why God is afflicting us. (We do not fully understand and never will in this life.) We should ask Christ to give us the grace to begin to see his presence in our lives and especially in our sufferings. With the eyes of faith and the Spirit's grace and gifts of wisdom, understanding, and knowledge, we can recognize the presence of Jesus. That presence is enough, although God in his mercy will not deny us some consolation. He is the Consoler of the afflicted, and he knows what we need.

I have certainly been consoled and strengthened by the experience of Christ's love in my life and by the signs that he is truly changing me. Still, I only see the surface of my life. Deep down God is working a wonder, and the means he uses penetrate my whole life, with its joys and sorrows and all that is yet unknown. Who knows the deep connections of love that wind through the mystical body of Christ? When I say to God each day, "I offer you everything," he gives over the energy of my small love in union with the cross of Christ, so that its power might sustain others.

When I give myself to God, he does with me what he wants. Here, too, I must grow in the trust that really enables me to let go and give everything over to God. When I offer him my prayers, works, joys, and sufferings, I usually offer an unspoken list of *preferences*: "O Lord, take my sufferings, and use them according to your will, *but* (if it is your will, of course) please don't make them any worse. In fact, take away this pain, make me able to use my talents, and—why not?—give me a few goodies, like maybe some more money (if it is your will, of course)."

I am not embarrassed to admit that this is what is in my heart when I pray. I am weak. Do you pray differently, really?

But I am beginning to learn what it is to trust in God. God knows I am weak. He knows I am a child. He is my Father. He is not just fooling around with my life.

After all, I don't play around capriciously with the lives of my children. I don't say, "Ha, ha, no breakfast today, because I want you to suffer and learn what hunger is!" If my children ask for bread, I don't give them stones. God is certainly a better Father to me than I could ever be to my own children (see Matthew 7:9, 11).

Why am I afraid that I can't trust him? Could I have really given myself a better life than the life that God has given me? And can I construct a better future for myself than what God has planned for me? Should I not trust him?

What God wants for me is much more, much greater, much more glorious and joyful than what I think I want for myself. In eternity we shall see all and rejoice in all. Here we see through that dark glass called faith (see 1 Corinthians 13:12). Sometimes it is very dark, but we must trust God to give us what we need to sustain hope and to grow in the capacity to respond to his mysterious love with our own self-abandoning love.

Let us not grumble. Let us seek the "rest" that Jesus promises to those who are weary and burdened (see Matthew 11:28). The Holy Spirit teaches us how to pray, in the depths of our souls and in the words of Scripture (Romans 8:26). Let us trust in his inspired lamentations, by which we pour out our hearts so that God might fill them.

Lamentations

Why do you stand afar off, O LORD?
Why do you hide yourself in times of trouble? (Psalm 10:1)

How long, O LORD? Will you forget me for ever?
How long will you hide your face from me?
How long must I bear pain in my soul,
and have sorrow in my heart all the day?...

Consider and answer me, O LORD my God;
lighten my eyes, lest I sleep the sleep of death....

But I have trusted in your merciful love;
my heart shall rejoice in your salvation. (Psalm 13:1–2a, 3, 5)

Be gracious to me, O LORD, for I am in distress;
  my eye is wasted from grief,

my soul and my body also.
For my life is spent with sorrow,
    and my years with sighing;
my strength fails because of my misery,
    and my bones waste away....

But I trust in you, O LORD,
I say, "You are my God." (Psalm 31:9–10, 14)

When the righteous cry for help, the LORD hears,
    and delivers them out of all their troubles.
The LORD is near to the brokenhearted,
    and saves the crushed in spirit. (Psalm 34:17–18)

CHAPTER SEVENTEEN

Offering Is Not Easy

Offering. When it comes to suffering, it is here that we arrive at the heart of the matter. That miserable feeling that suffering is a waste—that there is nothing worthwhile that I can do with it—is not really based on truth. If we believe in the cross, then we know that suffering is the supremely creative, constructive, transforming power in the universe.

At the heart of the life of the Church is the suffering Jesus, whose sacrifice is made present daily in the Eucharist. I am called to offer my sufferings in union with Christ on the cross and in the Eucharist, in reparation for my sins, for my own salvation, and for the salvation of the world. This is the most profound meaning of my suffering, and it is for this reason that God permits me to suffer. Not only am I called to cooperate with Jesus in being conformed to his saving death; I am called to cooperate in a mysterious way as an instrument of his saving power in the world.

In chapter nine I tried to express this in a meditation on the Morning Offering:

I offer you my sufferings,
that by your grace I might embrace them in faith and love
and bear them in patience, serenity, and Christian hope;
so that through them your Holy Spirit might lead me
along the secret paths of your compassion,
using my pain, weakness, and sorrows
as instruments of solidarity and saving strength
toward those—unknown to me—whom you seek to touch
in your unfathomable mercy.

I have this point nailed in both prose and poetry, right? Then why is this the hardest chapter for me to write in this entire book? Why do I feel at a loss for words here?

If this were a book on the theology of suffering, I could produce an extensive discourse on this point. (Perhaps someday I will write a book on the theology of suffering, but I am going to have to feel a lot better in order to muster up the energy for that project.) But this is not a book on the theology of suffering. This is a personal testimony. I wish to attempt here to express what it means for me, John Janaro, to offer *my* sufferings to God.

Am I the only person in the world who finds it *extremely difficult*—indeed sometimes incomprehensible—to "offer up" my sufferings? I feel as though I have no idea what this even means, or rather I should say that I cannot grasp in a concrete way how this deep Christian mystery relates to my actual sufferings.

It is easy to discourse about someone else's sufferings. It is easy to say to someone, "Offer it to Jesus," or, "See how much

God loves you," or, "How many graces you must be receiving!" Sometimes I tell people that suffering is just causing me to rack up more time in purgatory because of all the complaining that I do about it. In fact, what I mean to say is that suffering is hard for me. Of course it is.

We should remember this when we try to console and advise others in the midst of their sufferings. Offering our sufferings in union with Jesus *does not make them go away*. If I have pain, and I offer it to Jesus, *it still hurts*. And I still wish it would go away. Does this mean that I am not really offering it to God? Am I not doing it right?

This is not the point. If I say to God, "Thy will be done"—even if I say it with gritted teeth because I can't get it out any other way—then he begins to transform my suffering and to manifest his glory in me and through me. The saints ask for suffering in order to participate in God's redeeming love, because they have concretely penetrated the mystery of salvation and the mystery of sin, both within themselves and in the world. All Christians do this in some small way whenever they truly embrace a voluntary penance. But the value of suffering begins with (and always returns to) the yes we say to God in response to his concrete plan for us, as it actually unfolds in our lives.

As long as I somehow say, "Thy will be done," I can feel free to beg God to make me feel better, to deliver me from this problem or do whatever I feel that I need. God has a plan. He knows my weakness, and he will provide the consolation, respite, and comfort that he knows I truly need.

But the fact is that before I reach the end of this journey, I am going to have to suffer *more*—not less—than I do now. And that is true for every single one of us. Death is the ultimate suffering, because at that point we must surrender everything to God. This involves the suffering of self-abandonment. How will we find the strength to say yes to God when we are dying? Only by dying with Jesus: "Father, into your hands I commit my spirit" (Luke 23:46). He will pray this in and with each one of us if we let him. What a horror death would be without him.

Then there is purgatory to consider. Before I get to God, I am going to have to be perfected by suffering, one way or another.

Ultimately, however, the value of my suffering does not come from what I put into it. It is Jesus who suffers in me and through me. I belong to him, and it is his suffering that now grazes the edges of my life but will ultimately pierce through its very heart.

I am not scandalized by the fact that I am not very good at suffering. Suffering produces humility. It simplifies life. It teaches us patience. It teaches us what is really important. It is a grace that allows us to help others, to share their burdens, to be merciful to our fragile brothers and sisters. It heightens our sensitivity to the terrible evil in the world and to the coldness of human hearts that reject the love of God. In it we begin to share in the sorrow Jesus expressed over the world and the burning love with which he desires to save it. God gives us the grace to want to satisfy that burning love of Jesus, to grow to the measure of that love.

We also begin to glimpse those terrible dark places: human hearts without God, burdened with the horrible reality that we call mortal sin and not even knowing it; human hearts that are willingly seeking the darkness or who are oppressed by violence and can only bring forth violence in return. It is here especially where Jesus' pain reaches its greatest anguish. He loves each of these hearts, and he draws us into this love, too.

All of this awareness comes with time and in the measure with which God chooses to give it. I remain at the beginning of this mysterious road. I can say these things, and yet when it comes to my own trials, I seem to lose sight of the connections and start to flounder. My sufferings seem to be nothing but humiliation. I feel as if I am being crushed or suffocated. The voice of discouragement begins to creep in. There is always the danger of discouragement. But God's mercy is stronger than that, and I cry out to him.

Perhaps I am improving in how I handle suffering. I have begun to trust God because I have seen that he does not leave me alone. I think of that moment in Peter's life when, after beginning to walk on the water, he panics and starts to sink. Jesus reaches out and grabs him (see Matthew 14:25–31). When I am drowning, this is the one thing and the essential thing: *let him grab me.*

Jesus, I'm in Pain

Jesus, I'm in pain. What can I do?
Try to relieve the pain. Take my medicine.
The pain is still there.
What now?

Jesus, the pain never goes away.
I am always scratching at it.
Do you want the scratching?

Here. Take it.
Use it in your mystical way.

What am I offering you, Jesus?
Garbage from the excess of my life?
It's all trash:
the sore shoulder, trash;
the grouchy stomach, trash;
bad back, stiff knees, weak legs, trash;
headache, trash;
exhaustion, trash;
trash, trash, trash.

Do you want the slow-moving sludge of my day, Jesus?
When I feel miserable, I groan,
and the noise pours out of my mouth like vomit.
Do you want that?
My dragging feet—they would hurt less and look better
if I walked in love—but no,
I hurt,
and I drag extra
to show off my misery to other people.
I drag my leg along
so that it shudders in the presence of God,
as if to say, "Why is this affliction sucking the life out of me,
O God?"

Is this something I can offer to you?
Do you really want all my stupid thoughts?
the cheap shots at other people all day long?
and above all the pathetic self pity:

"I'm a sick man.... Doesn't anybody care?"
Do you want this life?

I offer it all to you, dear Jesus,
throwing myself upon your mercy,
plunging all of my absurd, awful life
into the fathomless depths of your mercy
because I believe in you,
and I trust in you.

Take the junk, Lord Jesus.
Take it all.
Do with it whatever you want.
Do with me whatever you want.

What remains is faith,
because you can do anything.
What remains is hope,
because you can
and you want to
clean up my mess.
What remains is love,
because you are so beautiful
in the midst of my broken junk.
You hold on to me in this life that I rebel against.
I rage and cry and wither,
and you don't want to go away.

PART THREE

Jesus Christ in a Suffering World

|

|

|

|

|

CHAPTER EIGHTEEN

Listen to Your Heart

What keeps me going? Why don't I just lie down and never get up again?

Sometimes I feel like shrinking beneath the covers of my bed. I feel tied to a wall with tight cords from head to foot. Then the cords loosen on the outside, but my brain is still knotted up inside, and all I feel like doing is falling down. Or with patience, carefully, in small spaces of time, the knots untangle and the cords slacken a bit more. I can write a few lines. I can write pages. But then the cords start digging in again.

I am trying to adapt to the rhythm of this, but of course I feel bound up, roped in, and confined to a small space. And even in that small space, I sometimes feel as if I am in the way— a burden to those who are stuck with the obligation of having to be bothered with me.

If I really thought that my value as a human being was measured by the way I *felt*, I think that I would find life impossible and wish that I did not exist. If my person were nothing but consciousness of pain, frustration, and disappointment, I expect that I would want to melt into oblivion.

How do people live without God? I am not surprised that sick people, living in misery in a world that says there is no God—that there is nothing but this life—are tempted by euthanasia or suicide. Why go on dragging yourself around like an old dried-up piece of meat in a world that has no meaning beyond physical vitality?

What amazes me is that people who do not know God do have the energy and desire to go on living. I think the only way to account for this is the fact that there *is* a God who cares personally for everyone—even those who do not yet know him or who think that they have rejected him.

God plants the seeds of hope in every human heart. If there were nothing but this life, then despair would be the logical human position, even for the healthiest of people. Yet the human person has to be *driven* to despair, as if it were against nature. People endure unimaginable misery *and keep going*. They do not feel that there is any reason to carry on, and yet they do. They have a sense that there is more than what they feel.

I do not think that billions of dollars are spent on health care just because people want to extend their miserable little lives a bit more before they are ground into nothingness by an implacable material universe. People have a tenacious sense—even if they are unconscious of it—that there is a path and that they are on it, that they are going somewhere and that they have to *keep going forward*.

What does this mean to me, a Christian burdened by circumstances but also blessed with the gifts of faith, hope, and charity?

I feel sick. That is not insignificant. It is a part of my path, a path I walk with Jesus. Does that make me feel better? Sometimes. But if walking with Jesus were nothing more than a pious sentiment designed to make me feel better (temporarily), it would not be worth much.

The point is that walking with Jesus *is the truth*; it is what constitutes the reality of my life. I do not always feel the truth of this, but I believe it. And as I walk with him—as I live this relationship with him—he strengthens my certainty; he builds up my life. He shapes within my soul the virtues of faith, hope, and love—making firm my conviction that he is with me on *my* path. If I stay with him, he will sustain me. This is what it means to live as a Christian. It means that I belong to Christ.

And because I am a Christian, something stirs in me and moves me to want to be a light to those who are stumbling along toward that which they do not know. I want to cry out, "Keep going! Keep looking, asking, groping. Cry out for help. The world is full of hucksters who try to put people's lives in boxes and sell them back cheap. Don't listen to them! You're not young, you're not satisfied, you're not good-looking, you haven't gotten what you want, you're disappointed, you're hurt. But you have a heart that whispers truth, goodness, beauty. You're angry and frustrated because you can't see any truth, goodness, or beauty. But your heart is *not* lying. Listen to it. It is a promise: "*You will not be cheated*. So don't give up."

No matter how I may *feel*, I know that this is true.

How can I be so sure? How can I be sure that you will not be cheated if you really listen to your heart and cry out for help and keep seeking? Because Jesus is real, and he loves you. He is right in front of you on the path, even if the fog prevents you from seeing him. He created your heart. He put the desire for truth, goodness, beauty, justice, love, and dignity within your heart. He *is* Truth, Goodness, Beauty; he is the Reality that every genuine impetus of your heart seeks. He is seeking you, and he wants you to let yourself be found.

Jesus is not a drug that helps dull my pain. Nor is he just my particular philosophy of life or support community—something that works for me but might not necessarily work for you. He is *for me* because I am a human being. That means he is *for you.* I am sure of this.

But how? Who do I think I am, anyway? What sustains this certainty in a blockhead like me? I haven't seen any miracles. I haven't had any visions. And it is definitely not that I have a deep spirituality: I am a spiritual wimp.

What makes me so sure that my ideas about the meaning of life are true for everyone? That is just the point: These are not my ideas. They are not vague ideals about goodness or the importance of Christian ethics or the value of suffering. I could never give myself this certainty, not even with all the philosophy of the ages.

It is Jesus, the objective, actual, true Son of God, the living man who is with us now, who makes me certain. He is here, in my life, in a relationship with me. In fact, he started it—not me. "In this is love, not that we loved God but that he loved us and sent his Son to be the expiation for our sins" (1 John 4:10).

And so I need to be with him. We all need to be with him.

CHAPTER NINETEEN

Redeemer of Man: A Meditation

All-holy and almighty God,
since the dawn of Creation
your wisdom has been visible
in the things you have made,
in the whole of that great, wide world
you gave to man, that he might praise you
and wonder at your vastness
and your power.
You have called every human being to seek you
through the capacity to affirm truth,
the desire for goodness,
the sense of justice,
the impetus to give one's self in love,
and the thirst for beauty
that you have inscribed deep within every human heart.

Man, however, has wandered far from you,
distracted by his own mastery over the world you have given
him.

He has forgotten you,
the Creator,
the secret glory at the heart of all things,
and has instead lost himself in his own analysis
of the bits and pieces of reality—
    trusting in his own small mind
    and constructing life according to his own mean and selfish
plans.

But you have not allowed man to abandon forever
the splendor
and the love
for which you made him.
You came in search of man.
You sent your only Son,
the Word—eternally begotten of the Father,
through whom all things were created,
in whom all things consist—
        the Word of Life!
        The Word made his dwelling among us.

Jesus,
by dying you destroyed our death;
by being lifted up you gathered man to yourself;
and you rose from the dead
as the New Man,
the Living One,
fulfillment of the promise
that God whispers in every heart
as he breathes life into the soul.

All-merciful and loving Father,
through him who died on the cross—
   surrendering himself to you so as to gather all who are lost—
breathe forth anew upon us
your healing and life-giving Spirit.
Turn our hearts once again to you, Father.
Make us your children, trusting in your provident love,
calling out to you with grateful affection,
turning to you in every need.

Let us rejoice in the beauty of your gifts
as we walk the road to your kingdom
in the love of your Son, our Risen Lord,
and in service to our brothers and sisters,
in whose faces we glimpse the glory of his face.

CHAPTER TWENTY

Christian Communion

Emmanuel, "God with *us*."

Throughout these pages I refer to "*my* relationship with Jesus" and "Jesus walking with *me*." It is truly a personal relationship. Being a Christian means being in *communion* with Jesus, the Savior of the world.

But this communion is not isolated. If I belong to Jesus, I am also united with everyone else who belongs to him, and I share with them in his mission of seeking salvation and bringing it to the world.

Perhaps this sounds rather vast and abstract. But it is not an abstraction; it is a *mystery*. A mystery is the transformation and expansion of reality that occurs when God—who is *the mystery*—intervenes in a special way in the circumstances of human history. The wonderful mystery of Jesus has generated in history a wonderful mystery that we call the Church—the presence, the hands, the heart of Jesus extended through space and time, reaching out to every place and every nation, seeking to touch every person in a *human* way, because Jesus is divine *and human*.

Jesus is in glory. He has triumphed over death and over the limitations and frustrations of this world. By his power the life and worship of the Church and also our own prayers and sufferings are mystical vehicles of his love in unseen places and in the depths of hearts. In another wonderful way the greatness of his glory is manifested in the manner in which he inserts himself into the ordinary rhythms, activities, and gestures of everyday human life and human interaction.

Jesus did not come into my life through some private and hidden communication (as I said, I have seen no visions). He came into my life through other people who were already walking with him. It began with those who brought me to the waters of baptism, and it continues through those who have taught me, those who minister to me as instruments of his grace, and those who accompany me and sustain me with their words, their testimony, and their friendship.

For two thousand years Christianity has been people in a relationship with Jesus and in relationships with one another. The relationships with one another have had their share of problems: abuse, manipulation, and violence, to name a few. That is not surprising. Pick any group of human beings in any place or time, and you will find such problems. The miracle that I have encountered in the Church is that, in the midst of all this human frailty, there is something else.

Above all there is Jesus himself, substantially present in the Eucharist. The greatest of mysteries—his crucified, risen, and glorified body and blood in his once-for-all infinitely loving offering of himself—is made present every day by his sacred ministers ordained to act as his instruments. These are men with personalities and struggles and flaws, and they need love just as does everyone else.

The Lord of the universe, mighty God, Prince of Peace, is right down the road from where I am sitting. I can visit him. (I want to visit him more often.) I can, even here where I sit, turn to him and focus my heart on that concrete presence, offer him my love and adoration, and pour out my sorrows to him. And I can receive him, my food and drink, my sustenance; thus he nourishes me and draws me into his life.

Some Christians find it hard to bear the "physicality" of the mystery of the Eucharist. But we believe that the infinite, eternal God became man and gave us his body and blood on the cross, so why should we shy away from the Eucharist? After all, it was his idea, not ours: "Take, eat; this is my body" (Matthew 26:26). "He who eats my flesh and drinks my blood has eternal life" (John 6:54). Those are his words, mysterious but wonderful. We embrace them as we embrace him, with an abandonment of ourselves and our own limited mentality, of our own calculations of what is possible and what is not possible for God. Only thus can our human hearts expand to participate in the life of the God who is Love.

Jesus also gives himself to me in and through the lives of his people. That means the people who are actually in my life. Through the years we have prayed together, worked together, eaten a lot of food together, carpooled, watched one another's kids, talked about our problems, prodded one another along, read books and watched films together, given one another money, and done all the other stuff that people do together. We have fought with one another, avoided one another, fibbed to one another, gossiped, bragged, and sometimes even hurt one another deeply. We have forgiven one another for many things.

There are many things we still need to forgive. We need to be healed. We are called to love everyone, to love the whole world. But we are especially called to love one another, because without this the other love is impossible. We are foolish people who need to beg for his mercy.

There is something else right in the middle of all this humanness. It is Jesus. Just the awareness of the fact that we are together because of him is unique. What else is there in the universe that can bring human beings together, continually renewing and sustaining the expectation of love before one another?

Let me express it in a personal way. I know that I can only find Jesus in the Church, which means the tradition, the teaching, the sacraments, the witness of the saints, and also the particular people who make up the environment of my daily Christian life. It begins, of course, with my wife and family, and then there are others. All that is most true and intimate in my relationship with Jesus has been given to me through people who have taught me to pray, who have pointed to what is important, and who have helped me bear my burdens.

When I say, "Jesus is present in my life," I know this not because of some private revelation but because someone *taught me* that this is true, with words but also with his own witness. When you see a person who is loved by Christ—when you spend time with that person and watch how he or she lives—the truth that "Jesus loves you" becomes more tangible, more convincing, more deeply rooted.

What I have received from others is much more than those others could have given me by themselves. If Jesus were not real, they could never have communicated realities that are so central to my life, that remain with me and change me. If Christians are just a group of people who get together because of a common interest in some old books and some rituals, then they are a rather sorry club. If Christians try to live isolated, individualistic relationships with Jesus and gather only to talk about Christian theology or spirituality, then they will be weak, at best.

But if Christians allow Jesus to work among them, that something else enters into the fabric of their personal lives and their life as a community. It is a foretaste of the kingdom, where God will be all in all.

That is why Jesus put us together. That is why he commands us, "Love one another as I have loved you" (John 15:12).

CHAPTER TWENTY-ONE

Ask!

There is a popular saying: "You gotta do what you gotta do." It is helpful for some people. It stiffens their resolve in the face of what is necessary, of what must be endured. I myself have found it helpful. But I have also found that it sometimes smacks me against the wall. I find myself saying, "I *can't do* what I gotta do!" What happens now?

Must I sink into the abyss? But sinking into the abyss is not an option. In our culture you can't even sink into the abyss without filling out the proper forms and applying to the appropriate bureaucrats. There is only one real possibility: *Ask for help*. Ask and keep asking. *Beg* for help.

What would happen if we all started asking one another for help—if we found the humility to turn to one another and say, "I can't do this on my own; I need you. Please help me!"? We would, in time, find ourselves inside a mysterious and wonderful experience: real human community.

Here is another saying: "God helps those who help themselves." There is truth in this—as long as we remember that we are children. If my three-year-old is trying to build something with her blocks, I will delight at how much she can accomplish, and I will also hold up the side if necessary or help her put a block in place. I am her father. I want her to grow and learn new things, and I also want to support and encourage her. God must see us this way.

But the saying hardly serves as a sufficient maxim. First of all, it emphasizes its clever paradox at the expense of clarity and conceptual precision. How, exactly, am I supposed to help *myself*? The very notion of *help* implies the need for something that I do not have already, something I need to receive from another. *Help* implies the contribution of another person and therefore the reality of relationship between persons.

Perhaps I think I am "helping myself" if I go out on my own and find the thing that I do not have. I would call that being resourceful. "God helps those who are resourceful"—certainly. This phrase is not as catchy, but it more accurately expresses the truth. God delights in our creativity and ingenuity, which manifest the intelligence and freedom that we possess in his image.

Nevertheless, we can surely say more about God's help than this. We emphasize the need for our own effort in order to discourage laziness. We can't just sit around and expect God to do everything for us; he is not a cosmic problem-solving machine. He is a Father who does not want his children to be petulant and idle slackers or spoiled brats.

If my three-year-old throws her blocks against the wall, I am not going to pick them up. She is going to pick them up, although if she is sorry and needs help, I will help her. She is, after all, just a little girl. And if she falls and hits her head on the table, I jump up and grab her. I make sure she is not hurt. I take care of her.

The truth is that God, our loving Father, helps those who *need* help—which is to say, *everyone*. He gives us the help we need in the way in which we need it, because we are his little children. "God helps those who help themselves" fails to resonate with the tenderness and dependence that our real relationship with God entails. Too often it is a pious mask for an attitude in which we see ourselves as self-sufficient and God's help as something extra, and indeed not even really necessary. But we are not self-sufficient. We need help.

It is especially true that "God helps those who ask for help." Jesus tells us: "Ask!"

What is God's help? It is his mercy.

There is no human person in the world who cannot ask God for mercy. No human predicament, no degree of moral and spiritual disgrace, is beyond the reach of God's mercy.

But what if you don't want God's mercy? There are some people who don't even think of it. For these people above all we must pray. But then there are people who actually say to themselves, "I don't want God's mercy!" If you are thinking this way, you have already begun—somewhere within yourself—to desire it.

Are you angry with the Lord? Bitter? Are you shaking your fist at God? Look at that little fist, that fist made up of human fingers. God loves that little fist of yours. I think my three-year-old's fist is the cutest thing, even when she is having a temper tantrum. And God your Father made your fist; he knows every line of every finger. He wants to uncurl those stubborn little fingers and hold your hand.

"But I don't know how to ask God for mercy!" *Ask* him to enable you to ask him for mercy. Wherever you are right now, ask him to show you his mercy and give you a heart that wants it. Everything good comes from him. So even if you look at yourself and say, "I am totally evil," you can turn to him and ask for a little drop of goodness, and he will give it to you.

"Ask, and it will be given you" (Matthew 7:7). What a simple promise! So, are you a sinner? Ask. Are you lonely and suffering? Ask. Are you debilitated by pain and physical humiliation? Ask. Are you a "good Christian"? Ask *more*, because there is the ever-present danger that you may have forgotten how much you need to ask. Are you a saint? Then you don't need me to tell you to ask because you have been asking for a long time. And you will continue to ask, from depths that I can't even begin to fathom. While you are at it, ask him to have mercy on me.

Thus he showers upon us his mercy, not to the demand of our measure and expectations but in response to our recognition that *we really need him*. Sometimes he seems to delay. This is because he wants us to keep asking; he wants us to experience our total need for him. Ask, keep asking, and never give up. You shall receive; it is a promise from God. "Whatever you ask in prayer, you will receive, if you have faith" (Matthew 21:22).

You really don't want his mercy? Well, watch out then, because he is going to come looking for you. Are you going to try to hide? He is, you know, infinitely clever. But he is a lover, not a bully. Love cannot be forced; it is freedom itself. Thus the mystery of evil entails the real possibility that we might succeed in escaping from his loving embrace forever. But we will not become free and independent by escaping from God's love. Outside of God's love there is nothing good, true, or beautiful. How awful.

So lift the cover from your hiding place. Turn to him. If you are still running away, then you haven't yet gone too far. Turn back and cry out to him. Ask for his help, his mercy.

God helps those who ask him. He even helps those who run away, as long as they don't refuse to come home. He helps those who do not push him away. He helps those who have been hiding from him, if they are willing to let themselves be found.

Do not forget God. Let yourself be found.

CHAPTER TWENTY-TWO

Family and Friends

I have five kids. When I feel up to it, I try to go outside and take a walk with the oldest four, in the afternoon, after school. I walk out the door. "Daddy!" they shout. "Daddy, Daddy, are you coming out?"

My children are still young—the oldest is only twelve—so they haven't reached the stage where they don't think it's cool to hang around with Daddy. So when I say, "Let's go for a little walk," everyone shouts, "Yeah!"

Small children are amazing. We think that we need to protect them from knowing about life's pain, but the truth is that children know—much more than we realize—how to put things in perspective. They have the instinct of innocence. A child can understand, and incorporate into his or her world, very profound things, as long as they are presented simply and directly.

"Daddy's not working right now because he is sick," the grown-up says.

The child might say, "He doesn't look sick."

And the grown-up can explain, "You can't see the sickness, because it is inside Daddy, but it hurts his arms and legs and head and all over his body, and it makes him very, very tired." Little children have no problem accepting that.

I must say, with gratitude to God, that I think my kids are pretty special. Sometimes they drive me crazy, but they are very good. Their mother deserves a great deal of credit for that.

So we walk up and down our little road. Everything has a kind of mythic permanence in the memory of a child. The street we live on or the little space under the bed in their room. My kids will remember walks with Daddy. There are blessings everywhere, in everything.

In comparison with my parents' generation, and even with many of my own friends, my wife and I married relatively late in life. I was thirty-three, and Eileen was twenty-nine. Both of us had pursued advanced degrees, traveled, and worked as teachers by the time God brought us together in the sacrament of marriage.

When my father was my age, I was already in college. My oldest child, John Paul, is twelve. Then there are the three middle girls: Agnese is ten, Lucia is eight, and Teresa is six. And then there is Josefina, whose first two and a half years of life could take up a whole book.

It is not unusual in today's culture to be a middle-aged man with young children. It is a bit unusual to be a middle-aged man with *five* young children. It has its challenges. In a few years I will have three teenagers in the house. God knows the trials that await us in these circumstances, as we lead and guide our children across the bridge to adulthood and to the discovery and taking up of their own vocations.

Belonging to a Christian community has made a great difference in our married and family life. Seeing my friends marry and raise children gave me the courage to love someone, share my life with her, and be open to the children God has given us. My friends have struggled with the challenge of their children's adolescence, but they have persevered and endured. Seeing how God has sustained them strengthens and supports our ability to trust in God for the years that lie ahead. We also have the companionship of families with young children, and their kids and ours are growing up together.

Our community is not hiding from the world in an enclosed village. We are living *together* in the midst of the world. The life of the Church provides the points of focus that bring us together. We share one another's joys, and we help one another in our struggles. We don't poke about intrusively in one another's lives.

My family has learned how much we need to depend on others not only through my struggles with illness. In 2006 my Lyme disease was in substantial remission. We hoped that this was the beginning of a permanent recovery. After much prayer and conversation, we became convinced that God had made it possible, and that he was calling us, to have another child. And so my wife became pregnant.

The other kids were excited. "We" were having a baby, they all said. I think we all were hoping for a boy, whom we would name Joseph. Saint Joseph has blessed our home and our family very much, and he never seems to want to take any credit.

There was virtually no indication that the baby would be born prematurely until the day I took my wife to the hospital. The birth was supposed to be in December, but it turned out to be a day in October. And the baby was a girl. Eileen and I decided right then and there to name her Josefina.

At the hospital a sonogram revealed that the baby's intestines had not developed properly. Josefina would require immediate emergency surgery at a larger hospital nearby. Given the circumstances, and the fact that we did not know what would happen next, I baptized her right away. The local pastor arrived a few minutes later and administered the sacrament of confirmation, which in the Western Church is given to babies only if they are in danger of death.

Soon this baby, barely five pounds and breathing laboriously, was placed in a mobile neonatal intensive care incubator. I recall feeling as if my little girl were being put into a large, incomprehensible, mechanical truck (needless to say, I thank God for that truck and everything else that followed). Thus she was taken to the large hospital, which had neonatal surgeons, specialists, and a neonatal intensive care unit (NICU).

During the surgery Eileen and I paced back and forth and prayed the rosary. We prayed to John Paul II (who may one day be the patron of intestinal surgery, among other things, since he himself had to undergo it after the shooting of 1981). The surgery was a marvel: The doctors found and connected the tiny portions of intestine.

This experience has given me hope that the instinct to cherish human life has not been utterly extinguished in our society. No effort was spared for our baby or for the dozens of other babies in the NICU, many of whom were in far more desperate conditions than our Josefina. How can such dedication exist side by side with the horrible assault on other little ones, those who are "unwanted"? We must pray for God's grace to open eyes and minds and hearts to the sanctity of all human life.

Josefina would need time to heal, and it would be a while before her intestines could function. Meanwhile she was fed intravenously. The staff told us she might be in the hospital for three weeks, and we could not imagine how we would be able to endure the separation. But Josefina had complications and eventually needed further surgery. The three weeks kept getting extended, until finally—after several months—the hospital stopped giving us estimates.

Every day my wife would drive to the hospital, an hour from our house, to spend the day with the baby. I was working, with increasing desperation and physical and mental exhaustion, so I saw Josefina only on weekends. It broke my heart to walk away, at the end of a visit, from that tiny helpless head with her enormous eyes. The doctors and nurses all fell in love with her. Indeed, people still fall in love with Josefina; she is a little ambassador of love.

Meanwhile our friends cared for our other children during the day. They picked kids up and took them where they needed to go. Then they made dinners for us in the evening. Eileen's mother came to stay with us several times, and she cared for the children. Everyone prayed. Whole cloistered convents were praying for Josefina. I wonder what God has planned for this child who has been loved so much.

After seven months Josefina finally came home with a feeding tube. She was barely ten pounds. But soon she was able to take a liquid formula with digestive additives by mouth, and slowly she began to grow.

Now Josefina eats and runs about and chatters away and makes trouble everywhere. She is like any three-year-old, except that she is small (which makes her that much more lovable).

She still has some occasional digestive difficulty, but we have every reason to hope that she will grow up normally. How grateful we are to God for this mercy. On some of my dark days she is a bright little light. I watch her and say, "Look at what God has done. Thank you, Jesus."

Our family still needs help. As Josefina became healthy, I became sick again. Our companions still care for us, and so do our parents. (I have learned that one never stops being the child of one's mother and father.) And this is God's mercy too.

CHAPTER TWENTY-THREE

Family Prayers

Families are meant to love each other. It is sad to see families broken or drifting apart in our culture. Is it because we have become so restless, busy, and complicated in our work, our possessions, and our desires? Or is it disappointed love?

When love is lacking in a family, there are wounds, and these, I think, are some of the hardest wounds to heal. It often seems that the pain cannot be completely relieved in this life. My heart goes out to all those afflicted with these invisible wounds. But God is rich in mercy, and he can heal them in time.

I have had a taste of the mysterious vulnerability of being a parent. How we love our children! We do not know, and we ultimately cannot control, the paths of their lives. We long to see them flourish. How much pain it gives us to see them in danger. This is our human nature, and the grace of God works within it to open us up to our total dependence on him.

Parenthood places us before eternity: A child comes forth from our flesh and goes forward to an eternal destiny. We stand before God with outstretched hands, begging for our children—for their lives, their health, their happiness, their need to belong to God. We beg together with our friends as we raise our children together. The parents of every generation, from the beginning of time, beseech God's mercy on their children in the great family that is the human race. We beg that one day we might all be with God and with one another, that the day will come when there are no more concerns, no more trials, no more wounds, no more tears.

Prayer for Parents

Loving heart of Jesus,
fountain of divine mercy,
for our sake you became a little child;
you, the Lord, the all-powerful one,
breathed softly,
frail and small,
in the arms of your mother.
You who hold all things in the world,
and for whom everything was made,
entrusted yourself
to the daily care
of Mary and Joseph.
You brought joy to a human home,
filled Mary's heart with wonder,
and were the light of the eyes of Joseph.
You knew the concern,
the trials and the toil,
the journeys,
the sorrows,

of Mary and Joseph
  as they worked to keep you safe,
  searched for you in your absence,
  fed you and clothed you,
  and rejoiced as you grew
  in wisdom, strength, and grace.

Lord Jesus,
you have entrusted to our care
these children
and given to us the burden
and the blessing
of making a home for them.
You who found boundless welcome
in the Immaculate Heart of your mother,
enlarge our hearts
that we might welcome our children
with love,
though we are not worthy
to have placed in our charge
these young ones:
  your brothers and sisters,
  whose only true Father is God,
  who have been called—each one—
  by an ineffable name
  and chosen by you
  to praise your glory,
  bathed in your redeeming love.

We are only your servants,
and our task overwhelms us.

How can we
till this garden?
Miracles of your love
shoot up and grow in our midst.
They turn toward us,
seeking the light of the sun.
And we feel so dull,
like shadows in the dusk
or the thick,
smothering,
blinding fog
of early morning.
Awesome and terrible
and too beautiful
this task:
we hold precious pearls in our hands,
bought at the price of your undying love.

Thus we kneel before you
and entrust ourselves, our children,
our home,
to your merciful heart.
Give us wisdom
to know what is good:
how to protect,
correct,
encourage,
and toil
for each of our children, for our family,
for our home.

Give us the energy of a love
that is delicate and strong,
full of the security of affection,
the light of discipline,
and the space of freedom,
leaving room for them to grow.

These children are yours,
and we are yours.
Grant that we might be a family,
dwelling in the love of your heart,
giving ourselves to you in one another,
finding your joy in one another.
   Joy!
   O Lord, keep always
   that treasure of joy
   alive in heart and memory,
   even amid the gathering of clouds.

Strengthen our family,
that we might be witnesses to your love,
that we might bear witness to your glory
and share your joy with our neighbors,
with the lonely ones,
with those who hunger
for bread
or love.
Make our home a refuge of comfort
to all who cross our threshold,
bearing their secret sufferings.
Give us strength

to labor day by day,
never discouraged,
seeking and finding in your mercy
water for the thirst of hearts
that love and struggle
and trust in you.

Prayer When a Child Is Sick
Lord Jesus,
I believe in you, and I trust in you.
My child is sick,
and I know that if you will it,
you can make her well.
I abandon her completely—
with my frail faith—
to your all-wise and all-loving mercy.
Your love is beyond all understanding.
  And I know
    that it may be the desire of that love
    to call her,
    now,
    to your eternal embrace:
though the sun has but risen
to enlighten her precious, sweet face.
  She is so new, so tiny, so tender.
  How recent is this joy,
    this light of our eyes,
    this warmth of life,
    this unrepeatable face:
      large-eyed, attentive

with the first stirrings of love
rising fresh from her little heart.

I am but a man,
weak, sinful, forgetful.
I entrust her to you,
and I plead for her healing.
She is yours,
and your glory is everything.
For this I ask faith,
   since your glory is too great
   and too distant
   for eyes made of earth.
And we are all little children,
newly taken from the ground.

I too am your child,
   still small
   and stumbling
   in the ways of faith and love and growing up.
It is thus, as a little child of faith,
that I place all my trust
in your compassion and mercy and pity,
and I beg you
to heal and make well
my little child.

CHAPTER TWENTY-FOUR

Little Things

I have begun to realize that life is not made up of a few big and dramatic sacrifices but of an innumerable multitude of small, unheralded sacrifices, day by day, hour by hour, minute by minute. Most of the time we either fail to give of ourselves in these little sacrifices or do so in a grudging fashion. Daily life can be irritating.

Or perhaps we hoard our sweet selves and cover them with a few prepackaged, meager sacrifices so that we can enjoy the satisfaction of feeling like a good person. Our mediocre routine negotiates its way around the challenges that demand real sacrifice. Daily life thus becomes comfortable—and secretly and safely boring.

To *sacrifice* means to give of myself. It is to love. It is, as the root of the word indicates, to "make holy" the circumstances of the moment that call out to me. It leads me to become holy, to become more like God. And what is God like? God is love. God gives himself. The human person, created in God's image, becomes his or her true self only by *giving* himself or herself in love.

Doesn't it all sound beautiful?

And here I am one afternoon, trying to take a nap. A kid comes in and shakes me. "Daddy, can I have an apple?"

"Yes," I grunt, and I try to slip back into a doze.

Two minutes. Another kid comes in. "Daddy, can I have an apple too?"

"Yes," I growl.

Soon there is a quarrel outside the room.

"He hit me."

"Well, you pushed me!"

"Daddy!"

Arrrgh! I said my kids were special, but they are still kids. This is my family, day after day after day....

The ordinary sacrifices of daily life—what a drag! But this is the school of love; this is where we learn to give. This is where God opens us up and draws us into that mysterious "giving away" of ourselves.

It is a challenge to go through the day without grunting and grumbling inwardly. The little things are exactly where we don't want to open up. It is easy to love in our imaginations or in the future. But it is hard to love today, because today is full of little things, and these are the real things.

How can we walk the road of daily sacrifice? Indeed, how can we learn to become *cheerful* givers? Do we believe that Jesus has made the one sacrifice that encompasses all our sacrifices? Do we believe that he really wants to make us holy?

Perseverance is first of all a matter of *faith*. I fail, and I repent, and I fail, and I repent day after day. I don't seem to be getting anywhere. But this is no surprise. I am weak. He will change me in his way, according to his plan, in his time. The great temptation is always frustration and discouragement. "Selfish," an evil voice whispers, "*that is the way you are. You are never going to change!*" The devil is trying to make me forget God.

No! What I need is God's saving and transforming love. I need to remember him, believe in him, adhere to him, and be forgiven again and again and again.

It all comes down to faith: Faith recognizes that he is here and that he has promised me the fullness of life and love. "He who believes in the Son has eternal life" (John 3:36). "In this the love of God was made manifest among us, that God sent his only-begotten Son into the world, so that we might live through him" (1 John 4:9).

Believe in him. Hold on to him. Trust in him. It is he who makes the little things into great love.

A Fool's Evening Prayer

I give you thanks,
Lord God,
for the abundant blessings
of this day.
I am above all grateful
for those few moments
when—by the gleaming light of your grace—
my small heart has been lifted up
in adoration and wonder,
in appreciation
and grateful recognition

of your constant, provident,
personal care for me,
soaking my faint spirit with floods of life
and raining down every goodness upon me.
And I beg pardon
for the hours upon hours
of this day
during which I ignored or forgot
your divine generosity
and lived in the midst of your joy
as though it were a dull routine.
Forgive me for being
a sour, hard, witless soul;
dumb like a stone, impenetrable
to the streaming torrents of your love.

CHAPTER TWENTY-FIVE

God's Love Is Real

Jesus loves us.

If we really grasped this fact, there would be no need to say anything further about it. Who would have thought that we could be loved like this?

I am just a little man, a brief spark flashing through ages of time, one of billions of little wiggly things on a small planet near the edge of a huge galaxy in an immeasurable universe. Still there is something in me that reflects the infinite mystery beyond everything, who creates and sustains everything.

The stars—immense, fiery things that they are—do not look upon each other. It is the little human being who looks upon the stars with wonder. It is the little human being who recognizes that there is a Someone beyond all things, and it is the little human being who recognizes that he or she too is a some-one—a *person* who is more like that infinite Person than any of the splendid, powerful forces that appear to be so solid and significant in the material world.

Still, what distance there is between us and the infinite One! Just look at yourself. You are not much higher than a bush. You have this odd-shaped head, with ears sticking out, arms and legs dangling. (Why just two of each? Why not six, like insects?) You sweat, you scratch, you blow your nose. Is there anything about you that is necessary to the cosmic order?

Is it not silly for us to strut about as though we were the masters of the universe? Yet we are blustery little buggers, aren't we? We bustle about, always searching for more, more, more. What if we could make ourselves gigantic, dazzling, deathless, titanic, with galaxies and supernovas like playthings in our hands? Even if we could succeed in making ourselves masters of the universe, we would face that same question: "What now? What more can I do? I want more!" And we would be no closer to that infinite Someone. We want that Someone, but how?

Could anyone ever have imagined what the infinite Someone actually *did* out of pure love for us? God became one of us—not as some abstract theory but as a man, in a particular place and time. If you think of it in purely human, worldly, or rationalistic terms, it is the most improbable thing imaginable. So many intelligent and even basically good people over the last several hundred years just haven't been able to swallow the whole thing. Jesus was a great teacher, they say, or a moral example, or a source of ideals for humanity. But surely he wasn't God!

Often when we say the Creed we don't realize how amazing the whole plan of God is from beginning to end. "Through him all things were made"—*all things*! He is the Creator and the sustainer of all reality.

And then what happened? Did he order us to worship, adore, and thank him from afar, burying our heads in the earth (so to speak), without hope of ever knowing him? If we look at the universe and the stars and the vastness of everything, we might be inclined to think that this is the only possible connection there could be between us and the infinite One who is beyond everything. But what *happened*?

"For us men"—that is, for you and me—"and for our salvation"—that is, because *he* loved us and *he* wanted us (even in our sins)—"he came down from heaven." Those are the words we use to express the miracle. "By the power of the Holy Spirit, he was born of the Virgin Mary."

Yes, this is a miracle: God was born of a woman; he *became man*. For seven hundred years the Holy Spirit protected this astonishing affirmation—true God, true man—from Christians who wanted to shave down or somehow tweak this mystery on one side or the other so that human beings could handle it.

But let us continue: "For our sake he was crucified under Pontius Pilate." That means that almighty God allowed some backwater governor to *judge* him. "He suffered, died, and was buried." The pagans of ancient Rome couldn't deal with this at all. "Surely," they said, "you mean that he pretended to die. It would be worthy of the divine One to fake out his enemies, but you can't really be serious if you say that God actually died!"

"On the third day he rose again" in a glorified and transfigured but still real and true human body, which he has joined to himself forever. This is enough. Could you or I or anybody else have made up this story?

Many people have tried to combine Jewish and Greek ideas or Eastern and Greek ideas, but they never came up with something like this. The myths of dying and rising gods that one might pull out of the rhythms of the seasons are like archetypal patterns, outside the realm of space and time. Even if we grant the point, along with Chesterton and Lewis, that the ancient myths were obscure and perhaps distorted hints at what was to come, the *historical reality* of the Resurrection is beyond human imagination and beyond any natural religious sensibility. It is what makes the whole Christian proposal impossible to accept without faith. We believe that the true God became a real man, died a bloody death, and really rose from the dead. These things actually happened.

Why did God do this? Because he loves us.

Saint Paul said that Jesus was "a stumbling block to Jews" and "folly to Gentiles" (1 Corinthians 1:23). We do not just adhere to one of many world religions, even given that our religion is true. We do not just affirm a bunch of theological ideas along with a moral code and a cultural tradition. The world we live in doesn't have any particular problem with a Christianity that so limits itself. The challenge comes when we affirm that God really did become man, really did die for us, and really did rise from the dead. And he did all this because he loves each one of us and *he wants us.*

Worldly reason is just never going to be able to wrap itself around the possibility that an infinite Being would get involved with us in this way. Saint Paul calls it "the foolishness of God," which is "wiser than men" (1 Corinthians 1:25). This is why the Creed is a profession of *faith*—the faith that becomes possible and effective through the love that God empowers us to give him in return. It is only love that can respond to love—the wild, wonderful, freely given love of God that comes to us in Jesus.

I know that I keep repeating this point, but it cannot be said enough: *We must grow in the love of God.*

God's action in the world is all about love: Creation, the permission of evil and suffering, the Incarnation, the Redemption, the Church. So it is with all the things that happen to us—our struggles, our joys, our aspirations, our disappointments, our relationships, our illnesses, our frustrations, our death. All things fail us in the end; love alone remains.

What do I mean when I say, "God, I love you"? In fact, as soon as I begin to ask this question, things start to get weird. I can spend hours groaning to God about how I do not love him enough and how I cannot bring myself to the attitude that he wants me to have. Mercy turns even this into something worthwhile in the end. I don't believe that any sincere attempt to communicate with God is ever *wasted*, regardless of our mood or our lack of understanding.

The fact is, I know little about the attitude God wants me to have, except that he is much kinder to me than I am to myself. Moreover, if I am frustrated by my inability to conform to God's will for me, it must mean that I care about his will. I recognize him and at least have the wish to be conformed to him.

But all of this is secondary. The reason why I miss the point is that I continually fall into the trap of assuming that everything begins with me. It is as though God were some great sleeping giant who won't wake up unless I make my love into a sufficiently loud noise (and become exhausted in the process). The truth is quite the opposite. My whole being is the result of Someone's saying, "I love you," at every moment. If it does not *seem* that way, it is still true.

What a marvelous thing it is to exist! And I cannot make myself exist. This reality called me must be a gift; indeed it is something treasured and cherished by Someone. I exist because Someone *wants me*. I am loved. To say, "God, I love you," is to respond to his original and perpetual "I love you. I *want* you."

God loves me. God loves you. We are not alone, ever. This is the beginning of the possibility of growing in love.

Did you make your hand, with its unique lines and blood vessels coursing through it, serving so many intricate purposes that you do not even understand and that you certainly did not invent? Look at that hand. Feel its organic pulsation, its warmth, its mobility. Catch yourself using your hand expressively. How can you possibly think that you are *alone*?

I know that I am not alone. I look back on forty-six years of life, and I find that almost everything I have experienced and everything that stands before me now are different from what I aimed for in all the striving and scheming and planning that motivated me through the years. All those expectations and all that analysis and all that grasping at life that have filled up my days have resulted in what?

You have heard the long tale of my trials and aches and pains and sickness. But I have so much to be grateful for in the years God has given me. My life is truly blessed. I know that suffering itself is the greatest and most precious of blessings, as is the grace to begin to bear it patiently and to recognize it as God's plan for me and the fulfillment of my vocation in the world. I struggle with this, but it is the struggle of faith working through love.

How wrong it would be to look at my life as one great temptation to discouragement. God's mercy shines in the ordinary good things—indeed the wonderful surprises—of my days on this earth. As I look back over the years, some things remain constant:

- I have been consistently and repeatedly foolish. My perspective on what I seek—what I think is going to make me happy—has been inevitably distorted or just plain wrong.
- I have expected either too much or too little or the wrong kind of thing from the given circumstances. I never manage to look things squarely in the face.
- I have achieved some of the things that I set out to do (for example, getting married and having a family, teaching, writing, and publishing), but these things are much better and much harder than I had ever dreamed, and in some ways they have a different significance than I once imagined—perhaps less inflated and surely with dimensions as yet undiscovered.
- There is definitely a Divine Providence that has guided me through everything (yes, *everything*). He has rescued me again and again from disasters that I might have gotten tangled up in if I were on my own. He is responsible for all the good in my life—sometimes with my half-witted, muddle-headed cooperation; other times in spite of my fury, frustration, and protest; other times through the slow and patient unfolding of events while I was vigorously and cluelessly scrambling around and anxiously looking for something else.

I am slowly (very slowly) beginning to realize how good God is. It has begun to dawn on me that Jesus Christ is actually in charge of my life. He has never failed me in anything. I can look at so much good and praise his mercy. Can I fail to trust his mercy in the spaces of life that still seem dark and heavy?

Jesus, I trust in you. I know that I will forget everything I have written here in five minutes and start fussing about something. But I will still remain in your hand.

CHAPTER TWENTY-SIX

Prayer of Trust

Jesus, I trust in you,
even in the turmoil of this night.
Oh, let me feel in its wild winds
the breath of your eternal lips,
  enlivening, expanding,
  spiriting dull flecks of my ashy ground
  into form, flesh, body
  of my New Eden everlasting.
For it is you who speaks to me,
you who calls me by name in each moment,
you who penetrates
the spaces within me that I do not know,
the moments of me
  not yet birthed by time
  nor conceived in the tiny gaps and crevices of my mind,
  nor even beginning to trace dim shadows
    before my near-blind eyes.

It is you who sees me,
you who grasps my hand and guides me
in the valley of shadows.

For you have taken every hollow trench
and scaled every slope,
   to stand in the fiery sun that has burned me.
You have won the victory
that you proclaim and celebrate each moment,
each day,
when you call my name,
when you call me to awaken
   to the frail pieces of light
   and gray dust of earth's every morning.

Save me!
For only you know me.
Shut my eyes and stop my ears
from phantom shades who cry out:
   "Your name is slave,
   your name is fear,
   blackness is your life."

Jesus,
you call my name.
Oh, open my ear that I may hear your voice clearly,
for you carry whole, within your living light,
the only me that will ever glimmer and shine—
   pool of light,
   like a splendid diamond

clean and cut
with the lines of your face.

You call me by a name never spoken before
and never to be uttered again.
My real name:
sounding like song and gushing—
   fresh, cold, sweet water of life,
   that rises up from the deep,
   deep well
     of mercy's hidden spring.

Let me live, O Lord, by faith—near blind, near deaf,
   straining the ear of earth to hear the echo of my name
   in gifted speech of hinted truth,
   though shallow like shells:
     child, beloved, likeness, your glory,
       your glory.
Lead me,
by the glory that slips between the crack
of faith's eye,
   to trust in you,
   to spy the promise of all made new.
Grant me that glimpse,
faint,
firm,
of all earth's pain and weight,
of my fighting, faltering,
fumbling heart's hope
   washed in white wonder.

PART FOUR

Lord, Teach Us to Pray

CHAPTER TWENTY-SEVEN

The School of Prayer

Praying means lifting up our minds and hearts to God. Most of my prayers are not very hefty. When I say them with sincerity, the very intention and effort are the beginnings of that focus on God. And God in his mercy does not reject my poor prayers when my mind and heart—in their faltering efforts to adhere to God—swirl with a hundred other concerns and ache to finish and get back to their hungry preoccupations.

But God wants us to grow in prayer. Suffering and tribulation are a school for that. When we are sick, we often don't feel that the quality of our prayer is improving. In fact, it can seem quite the opposite. When I am in pain, or in depression, or in obsessive fear, my mind feels as if it's tied in knots. I can't lift it to anything, much less God.

The problem here is that I think of prayer as a monologue, a speech that I give to God. I must tell him, as clearly and eloquently as possible, what I need from him and—of course—how much I love him.

Certainly, if one has been given the gift of words, there is nothing wrong in fashioning those words into an offering to God—to sing his praise with all one's skill. Much of this book reflects my own efforts in this regard. But everyone should realize that the prayers and reflections crafted herein have been written, generally, during periods when I was feeling pretty good. When I feel sick I am reduced to inarticulate groaning.

From a human point of view, I am very frustrated by this. But this frustration is a good thing. God wants me to be quiet and listen to him.

Prayer is conversation with God, and it is God who initiates the conversation. That does not mean that we should wait until God starts speaking inside our heads. He is always speaking, calling to us, drawing us to prayer. He speaks to our hearts. We begin to hear him when we become more aware of our need for him. This is where prayer begins: when our hearts cry out, "Lord, have mercy on me!"

We always need mercy, but the awareness of that need arises and intensifies when we are suffering. One of the things that has helped me see the mercy of God at work in my own suffering is the fact that it *has forced me to shut up and listen*. The ear of the heart that hears God has a very simple shape.

The cry of that heart is also simple: "Help. Have mercy on me. I need you." We may not be able to articulate these words, but that inward groaning that seeks him is the foundational response to the love he continually offers us.

We are dear to God in our weakness. He is close to us when we are suffering. He lifts us closer to him if we allow him to enter inside of that need that groans within us. He shapes us, in his way and in his time. He develops within us a mysterious dialogue that gives intensity and real value to whatever words we manage to say.

And we don't need to make up the words. Jesus has given them to us:

> Our Father who art in heaven,
> Hallowed be thy name.
> Thy kingdom come.
> Thy will be done,
> On earth as it is in heaven.
> Give us this day our daily bread;
> And forgive us our trespasses,
> As we forgive those who trespass against us;
> And lead us not into temptation,
> But deliver us from evil.
> (Matthew 6:9–13; see Luke 11:2–4)

This was Jesus' response to his disciples when they asked him, "Lord, teach us to pray" (Luke 11:1). The disciples realized that they needed to *ask* him to teach them how to pray. Jesus wants us to ask and to receive from him the prayers handed down through the living community of the Church. Thus he teaches us, and thus we learn to lift our minds and hearts a bit higher because we want to be closer to God. After all, where else can we go?

Our efforts to draw closer to God in prayer—that desperate, begging prayer in which the mind and heart taste the need for God—are important above all because they open us up to him. He is thus able to work a secret and mysterious transformation in our souls by which we grow into the persons he wants us to be for all eternity.

Prayer is a dialogue in which we live our relationship with

God. But God's part is always the greater one. He seeks us with an ardor infinitely greater than the small and distracted love with which we seek him.

"Thy kingdom come! Thy will be done on earth as it is in heaven." The twists and turns of life that make no sense to us are all part of his plan to open us up, forgive our sins, raise us higher, and bring us to the place where the seeds of eternal life will be nurtured and will grow.

CHAPTER TWENTY-EIGHT

All Things Are Possible

Jesus told the rich young man to sell all he had and follow him. If only the rich young man had not turned away, *sad*, because he had many possessions (see Matthew 19:26–22; Mark 10:17–22; Luke 18:18–25). If only he had cried out to Jesus: "Lord, *how* am I going to do that? I really like all of my nice stuff!" That would have been the beginning of everything for him. Jesus could have worked miracles out of that *how?*

Even a frustrated, confused, angry *how?*—as long as it is a real question and not a put-off or a self-justification—carries a glimmer of awareness that Jesus is *worth* whatever he asks of me or whatever burden he lays on me. I want to stay with you, Jesus. How? Help! I do not want to turn away from the face that looks upon me and loves me.

Of course, we do not know what happened in the end to the rich young man. Maybe he forgot about Jesus and joined the Pharisee party; after all, they kept the commandments just as he did, and he could sell just 10 percent of his stuff and still impress everybody by dumping sacks of money into the temple treasury. Or maybe one day he remembered the face of Jesus and that look of love and went out again in search of him. (That "look of love" is God's gaze within the depths of the heart, which is the beginning of the dialogue of prayer, the beginning of the vocation to eternal glory given to each of us.) He had turned away from Jesus, but Jesus had not turned away from him. "With God all things are possible," Jesus told his disciples (Matthew 19:26). Maybe the rich man found the face of Jesus again in the faces of his disciples.

Never give up! Stay in front of Jesus. It would be better to wake up every morning and say, "God, help me because I'm such a jerk!" than to forget God and shrink to the level of what you think you can do by yourself.

CHAPTER TWENTY-NINE

The Mother of God

Christian tradition tells us about a wonderful person who is a great friend and companion for me and for you. She is so full of God that there is no way she could possibly interfere with our relationship with him. She is God's living reflection, a luminous passageway right to the tender heart of her Son. In her we find the place where his humanity dwells.

Jesus gave this friend to us and us to her from the cross. There are no exceptions. Everyone belongs to her in a personal and particular way.

Let us not allow ourselves to be troubled by the problem of how one woman could love me and you and him and her and every person with intimacy and attention and a single-hearted care, focus, and compassion. It is a mystery of God's grace and a mystery of love. We have experienced the aspirations of love in our own hearts (and many of us too have experienced the limits and the illusions of human love left to its own resources, a love helplessly broken into fragments, a love that fails in its own energy—beginning in flame but ending in ashes). But we believe that God himself took our frail nature and, with his human heart, wrought miracles of inexhaustible love. And so it is God who empowers the woman to know and to love each one of us.

Let us then believe that *she really loves us*, that our relationship with her is more profound and more *solid* than any friendship we may have with people we can see and hear and touch, that it is real because God makes it real. Indeed, how could his human mother—who was the *first* one to believe in him, the *first* to receive that favor (*charis* or grace) of God that fulfills the Law—have no interest in *us*, with whom he has bonded himself forever as a brother, as the firstborn? Transcendent, *super*natural in every sense, and yet at the same time truly, totally, intimately human—such is the relationship that each of us has with the woman whom Jesus, as he gazed down upon her from the cross, gave to be our *mother in the Spirit* (see John 19:26–27).

Do not be afraid of Mary. Do not think of her as a collection of religious doctrines that we have to find a way to incorporate into the comfortable coherence of our system of thought. If we view a personal relationship with Jesus Christ as some kind of mechanical engine that produces our salvation, Mary will seem like a superfluous part. Where exactly does she go? How does she fit into the salvation machine?

Sometimes people say to me, "I have a problem with Mary." I reply, "Don't worry too much. You may have a problem with Mary, but she doesn't have a problem with you."

Jesus is the Savior of the world and the Lord of all creation, and his heart of mercy drenches us with torrents of love. Mary is a gift of the depths of that love. She is our first and greatest companion in that communion that is the Church: She brings us to Jesus and walks with us as we walk with him.

Do I really want to learn how to pray? Mary will teach me, through the Holy Spirit, in that great family that is the Church. Many earthly mothers teach children their first prayers; they teach them to say "God" and "Jesus" with reverence. Perhaps we adults think that we know all this. Personally, I feel that I still need help if I am to say those words in a meaningful and loving way.

Pray

How do I pray?
Pray to God.
But where is God?
I don't see him.
I don't feel him.

Who is God?
Jesus Christ.
Jesus came to reveal the face of God.
Jesus will hear my prayer.

But where is Jesus?
I cannot find him in the marketplace.
I cannot find him in the fields.
I cannot find him in the city.
He is in the Church, but hidden,
and my faith is weak.

Who knows Jesus?
Who can bring me to him?

Who has never left him?
Who was there at the beginning?
and the end?
and the new beginning?

Mary, you are standing next to me.
You have been with me from the beginning.
You will be with me at the end.
Mary, how can I pray?
Mary, pray for me.
Pray with me.
Teach me to pray with you.

CHAPTER THIRTY

A Meditation on Entrusting Ourselves Totally to Mary

Immaculate Heart of Mary,
merciful mother,
mother of tenderness and compassion,
I am all yours, and all that I have is yours.

O pure virgin,
immerse me in your immaculate heart.
Open my heart to receive Jesus.
For I am weak and sinful, and without you, Mary,
holy mother,
I cannot know the true face of your Son.

Obtain for me the presence and the power of the Holy Spirit—
he who transfigures and illuminates the whole of your being.
Through your never-failing intercession,
obtain for me his efficacious grace,
and bring his precious grace to me.

You are the Mediatrix—you who watch, and plead, and care for

the needs
of every human person redeemed by your Son,
with an ineffable attention, solicitude,
and tenderness born of the heart
of the mother of the living,
the heart that says to every person
in every moment,
"My child!"

O Mother, whose heart has endured the cross of my sins
and rejoiced in the promise of my resurrection
in the mercy of your Son;
O Mother, who draws me close
and calls me "my child,"
bring every gift, every light, every grace,
into the intimate depths of my heart.

Through your intercession
and the tenderness of your maternal love,
draw me throughout each day
closer to Jesus—to a real knowledge and love for him
as my Savior and Lord,
as the true Lover of my heart.
And help me to trust you completely
as a loving mother who watches over me
at every moment with a compassion
that can never be shaken.

Holy and merciful Mother of God,
stay with me, every moment of every day;
never leave me;

always find me, carry me, teach me like a tiny baby
every step that Jesus wishes me to take.

And in the final moment of my life,
when I stand in nothingness and total need,
obtain for me from the infinite mercy of God
the gift of the grace of final perseverance,
the gift of grace—which I can never earn—
to enter into God's presence
and be found worthy to enjoy his eternal glory.

Protect me from every evil.
Above all protect me from sin.
Obtain for me the grace
to adhere to God, to abide in him,
and in times of trial and temptation to choose him
and what leads to him,
to reject anything that might separate me from him.
Never let me separate myself from him by mortal sin,
for I am weak, foolish, and sinful,
and without him I am lost and can do nothing.
Obtain for me the grace to grow in love and holiness.

Immaculate, loving, tender heart of Mary,
I abandon to you my work, my future, all my hopes.
Intercede for me, that everything may happen according to the
wisdom of God's plan.
You know my heart.
You know my yearning.
You know my suffering.
I cry out to you with all my afflictions.

Help me, Holy Virgin.
Heal the afflictions of my body.
Free me from the prison of fear.
Obtain for me the true freedom for which my spirit yearns.
Provide for the material needs of all those entrusted to me.
Take care of my beloved family and all my loved ones in every way.
Make us merciful and full of love.

Holy Virgin, Mother of God,
Mary, Immaculate Heart of Mary,
my mother,
who never stops saying, "I love you,"
I place all my trust in you.
I love you.
I am all yours, and all that I have is yours,
my queen and my mother.

CHAPTER THIRTY-ONE

The Eucharist

Jesus has promised to remain with us always, and in the Eucharist he has accomplished an astonishing gift of himself: He has become our sustenance, our food and drink. The mystical banquet has begun, and Jesus is with us, but he takes the *lowest* place. What a great throne we would expect for the Bridegroom, and instead he has taken a hidden place, to the point that we might forget his presence.

But here is his secret: In becoming so small and so subject to us that we can take, eat, and drink him, he can give himself to each one of us completely as the Son of God who lives as glorified man, with a real body and real blood. Moreover, as *food* he can be present for each of us in a way that accords with our needs, because our hunger for the Bread of Life is never fully satisfied on this earth. He comes into our midst in the Eucharistic banquet, and he *remains* with us in a place reserved for him, even when we are not celebrating the sacred liturgy. Knowing that we are constrained by the necessities of daily life from being continually gathered in public worship, he wishes to remain nonetheless, so that none of us need ever want for his nourishment: "He who comes to me shall not hunger" (John 6:35).

The tradition of the ancient Church was to set aside and preserve in the house of worship a portion of the Sacrament so that the Eucharist might be available to those who are sick. Today we must ask, "Who among us is *not* sick? Are we not all in need of healing?"

We would be ignorant of Christ—indeed, ignorant of love—if we ever thought that we had been nourished enough by the Bread of Life. In the Eucharist Jesus remains among us in his paschal mystery (which is the foundation of our life and our hope), and any encounter with the Eucharistic Lord offers the possibility of being touched, nourished, and healed by the love that is given for all time in the words "Take, eat; this is my body.... Drink, ...for this is my blood of the covenant, which is poured out for many for the forgiveness of sins" (Matthew 26:26–28).

Each of us is, in some sense, one of "the sick" for whom the Eucharistic mystery remains available at every moment in the heart of the Church. The transformation of our lives is founded upon baptism: We are freed from the sin that separates us from God; we are healed, in a radical sense, and taken into the life of God as his adopted children. Yet we retain the scars of our broken humanity, evident in many ways. If we are not to succumb to our weakness and frailty, we need the divine physician and the medicine of immortality.

Indeed, in the measure that faith and love grow within us, so also shall our ardor to receive Jesus in Holy Communion and to worship him, love him, and hunger for him in every moment. Even at those times when I cannot receive him or be present to him in worship, I can hunger for him, seek him, and call upon him. I can go to the place where he has been set aside for me, because I am one of the sick who need him, and I can sit before the place where he is kept and open my hungry heart, so that he who fed the multitudes can take pity on me.

Even if I am somewhere else, engaged in the stuff of daily life, I can hunger for Jesus, seek him, and call upon him in the Spirit, conscious that his love, healing, and nourishment are always present for me in the sacrament of his Body and Blood. For this is offered for me and is even now kept in a special place for me, to heal my sickness.

Short Prayers to Jesus in the Blessed Sacrament

Jesus in the Blessed Sacrament, I adore you.

Jesus in the Blessed Sacrament, I love you.

Jesus in the Blessed Sacrament, glory to you.

Jesus in the Blessed Sacrament, sustain me.

Jesus in the Blessed Sacrament, nourish my heart.

Jesus in the Blessed Sacrament, I hunger and thirst for you.

Jesus in the Blessed Sacrament, I long for you.

Jesus in the Blessed Sacrament, I am nothing without you.

Jesus in the Blessed Sacrament, unite me to yourself.

Jesus in the Blessed Sacrament, never let me be separated from you.

Jesus in the Blessed Sacrament, embrace me.

Jesus in the Blessed Sacrament, love me.

Jesus in the Blessed Sacrament, hold my life.

Jesus in the Blessed Sacrament, by your risen flesh carry me forth from the tomb of my sins.

Jesus in the Blessed Sacrament, walk with me in the valley
of the shadow of death.

Jesus in the Blessed Sacrament, live in me.

Jesus in the Blessed Sacrament, love through me.

Jesus in the Blessed Sacrament, take away my stony heart.

Jesus in the Blessed Sacrament, give me a new heart.

Jesus in the Blessed Sacrament, go forth in my heart into the
world.

Jesus in the Blessed Sacrament, show your mercy through me.

Jesus in the Blessed Sacrament, find your lost sheep through
me.

Jesus in the Blessed Sacrament, gather your little ones through
me.

Jesus in the Blessed Sacrament, care for your own, whom you
have entrusted to me.

Jesus in the Blessed Sacrament, show compassion through my
heart to those around me who are most in need of love.

Jesus in the Blessed Sacrament, you are my joy.

Jesus in the Blessed Sacrament, refresh my soul.

Jesus in the Blessed Sacrament, cool my arid heart with your
heavenly dew.

Jesus in the Blessed Sacrament, I am lost without you;
lead me in your ways.

Jesus in the Blessed Sacrament, I am blind without you;
enlighten me in your truth.

Jesus in the Blessed Sacrament, without you I stand at the
abyss of death; save me.

Jesus in the Blessed Sacrament, without you I cannot love;
save me.

Jesus in the Blessed Sacrament, let me eat and drink and love
and live forever.

|
|
|
|
|

CHAPTER THIRTY-TWO

Reflections on the Mystery of the Eucharist

He Loved Them to the End

Beloved Jesus, I adore you.

Here is your love

to the end,

to the silence,

to the smallness,

to the inside of every moment.

This is your glory:

love inexhaustible

poured out in earthen vessels;

love Creator of the burning stars;

love Creator of the angels—

those great, gigantic, magnificent, comprehending spirits.

Love Creator of man,

master of the earth and its things

yet a tiny speck under the sky;

image of God,

dust and ashes,
great and miserable,
hungry man, hungry with a thousand hungers.
Beloved Jesus, I adore you.
Here is your love;
here is your glory:
love inexhaustible
poured out in earthen vessels;
love beyond all measure
become a morsel of food and drink
in our tiny mouths,
given and given, broken and poured out.
Glory to you, Love eternal!

Prayer Before Communion
O Lord, I am not worthy
to partake of these holy mysteries
of your Body and Blood.
Still you present yourself before me,
longing to embrace me;
you humble yourself—you,
Lord of heaven and earth,
Creator,
glory,
fire beyond the gaze of men,
before whom the angels veil their faces.
You wash my feet;
you become my food and drink.

O Lord, I am not worthy
that you should come under my roof.

I am weak and sinful.
Grant that I might not be slow
to believe the promises of my God.
Though I am nothing, I believe in you;
I believe in the ineffable love
through which you empty yourself
so as to raise me to your fullness.

I approach you in this faith,
in the hope it gives me,
and in the desire to love you
according to that share in your own love
that I pray the Spirit of your Father
may instill and increase within me.
Open the eyes of my faith
to recognize you in this simple gesture,
this supper,
this breaking of bread—which is your breaking
and giving
and giving away of yourself
in love without measure.

Open my heart
that I may receive you worthily and fruitfully;
live in me and sustain me as I am broken this day,
that I might not be scattered to the wind
but given away in love, my Lord Jesus,
unto eternal life.
Amen.

Thanksgiving

Lord Jesus,
Bread from heaven
falling,
lying lightly
on my grainy sand,
transform my desert wasteland
into great spaces
shining with your celestial Bread.
Strike the hard, dry stone in me,
that living water might rush forth upon a deathless thirst—
flowing in the wilderness,
irrigating,
new-creating,
living water changed to wine,
Body given—Bread of Life, cup of blessing, blood divine,
fruit of you, the tree, the vine
in my garden,
where you call, and I no longer fear your voice;
where your mighty wind brings the cool of the day:
refreshment,
gladness,
oil, unction,
covering lacerations that are no more,
drawing out the endless pain,
when at last I am freed from blame.
I thank and praise your glorious name.

The Grain of Wheat
Jesus, Living Bread,
hidden love, secret gift.
Jesus, you, the only you:
reaching, gazing, drawing near,
touching, entering the deepest place
through lips and mouth
as holy food.

The bread we break,
the grains of wheat,
fruit of the earth and work of our hands,
by your word the Bread of Life,
Jesus, you, the only you.
Your risen body, everlasting—
transfigured Love lifted up
to longing eye and yearning heart
under humble signs, veils
of the glory in which Love humbles himself.
Jesus, you, the only you.
The Bread, the food,
the grain of wheat fallen
into our little earth—
into our little sorrow, joy, work, hope;
into our little frustrations, bitterness, vanity, suffering;
into this curving, confining space—
buried with us, your chosen dwelling place!

Into our breathless earth,
down deep into fallow souls,
shriveled soil, grown barren

from the dense, heavy weight
of so much unoffered love.
Jesus, you, only you!
O Lord Jesus, come!
Burst the ground of my heart
with a harvest of abundant fruit.

CONCLUSION

It is fitting for these reflections to end with the Eucharist. My verses have little worth, but the Eucharist is God's poetry. Here is the Bridegroom's love song, where he begs his beloved, "Take me. Let me enter into you completely. Let me love you and give myself to you."

The relationship between mercy and suffering reaches an astonishing point in this moment. It is, if I may speak this way, as if God is begging me to have mercy on him! He thirsts for my love. Can I find a drop of my dry little self to place on those begging lips?

God has become one of us because he wants us to see how much he loves us. What are all our sufferings in the end? They are the reverberations of his great heart suffering because of the smallness of our love. He is on the cross begging us to love him. Still he knows us, and he knows how slow we are. He waits for us and calls out to us all through the "three hours" that are the span of our lives. Here he shows his mercy; he is the gift of the Father's mercy; he gives the One who is love and mercy, the Holy Spirit who transforms us into his lovers.

And so we pray to God our Father: "For the sake of his sorrowful passion, have mercy on us and on the whole world."[1]

Let us no longer deny him what his heart so ardently desires: our selves! This is the great marvel: God not only wants us to belong to him; *he wants to belong to us!* The omnipotent God *begs* you to let him belong to you. He is the Lover who pleads with you to say yes, that he might give his heart completely to you. He wants to be *yours* forever.

Go to him! Take up the crucifix: Look at him. He did this to make you whole and free and worthy of him, so that he might love you, give himself to you, and fulfill his longing for you.

Are you a sinner? *Look again at him on the cross.* His mercy cries out, "You don't have to be a sinner anymore." Give him your sins. Let go of them. Let him take them. He *is* mercy. He *will* hold you, bring you through the struggles, and make you free.

Go to him in the Church, in the sacraments in which he reaches out to you. Baptism is the beginning of a whole new life. Hear the voice of his mercy in the sacrament of reconciliation. Let him give himself to you in the Eucharist, where he will nourish you and fulfill his desire to belong to you.

Go to him in your spouse, your children, or in the person whom you know is in need of your love. Go to him in the depths of your own sadness, which belongs to him, for he claimed it on the cross. You must let him suffer your pain and create within it a space for love.

This book will fall to the ground and return to the dust, along with all our sorrows and the whole of this passing age. But his mercy endures forever. Go to him!

−Good Friday
April 10, 2009

NOTES

Chapter Eleven: In the Hands of God

1. John Henry Newman, "Sermon 2: Obedience Without Love, as Instanced in the Character of Balaam." See www.newmanreader.org.

Chapter Sixteen: The Lament

1. Cited in Sebastian Vazhakala, *Life With Mother Teresa* (Cincinnati: Servant, 2004), p. 37.

2. Edward Le Joly, *Mother Teresa of Calcutta: A Biography* (San Francisco: Harper, 1985), p. 321, cited at speroforum.com.

Conclusion

1. From the Chaplet of Divine Mercy. The Lord appeared to Saint Faustina Kowalska, a Polish nun, in the 1930s and instructed her in this devotion. See ewtn.com.

ABOUT THE AUTHOR

John Janaro is associate professor emeritus of theology at Christendom College, and currently a writer, researcher, and lecturer on topics related to religion and the humanities. He is a member of the Catholic lay movement Communion and Liberation and a frequent contributor to *Magnificat* magazine. He and his wife, Eileen, live in Virginia with their five children.